Indiana Wesleyan Methodist Youth Society Reading course book - 1993-1994

Robert Sayers Sheffey

Rev. W. H. Simpkins holding Brother Sheffey's saddle bags and sheepskin.

Story Of

The Life Of

ROBERT SAYERS SHEFFEY

A Courier Of The Long Trail—God's

Gentleman—A Man Of Prayer And Unshaken

Faith

By

WILLARD SANDERS BARBERY
Pastor Methodist Church

ISBN 0-88019-005-1

Schmul Publishing Co., Inc.
Wesleyan Book Club   Salem, Ohio

"The path of the just is as the shining light, that shineth more and more unto the perfect day."

"They that be wise shall shine as the brightness of the firmament; and they that turn many to righteousness, as the stars forever and ever."—Daniel 12:3.

Dedicated to

STELLA MAE BARBERY
My Wife

and

RITA JUNE BARBERY
Our Daughter

and

My many friends who, through their contributions and assistance, have made possible the publication of this story.

Preface

Southwestern Virginia has produced great men in every walk of life—soldiers, statesmen, and scholars,—but no man has lived between Roanoke and Bristol and between the Blue Ridge and Flat Top mountains who has made a deeper impression on the whole people of that part of the state than Rev. Robert Sayers Sheffey. I have been interested for many years in the hope that a biography of this man should be written before all of the generation that knew him personally had passed away. In 1907 Oliver Taylor, of Bristol, and myself began to gather data for such a book, but we learned that Edward Sheffey was also gathering materials on the life of his father and we gave up our plan for the book feeling that the work should be left to his son. No such book was ever printed, and Mr. Sheffey passed on to his reward several years ago.

I have encouraged and given small aid to Rev. W. S. Barbery, Methodist minister, in his effort to preserve some of the record of this strange preacher who as a man of prayer was during his life-time held in fear and reverence more than any man ever living in the New River, Holston, and Clinch Valleys.

Many have written stories about Brother Sheffey, but they consisted almost entirely of the peculiar things he did, and he was a peculiar man. When I was a boy around Marion, Virginia, I remember hearing a story about a conversation that took place between the preacher and his brother, Judge James Sheffey. The judge said to him, "Bob I want you to stop being so peculiar." Brother Sheffey answered, "I won't do it, for the Bible says that God's people are a peculiar people." "Yes," said the judge, "but there is no sense in being childish." "Yes, there is," answered the preacher, "for the Bible says that except ye be converted, and become as little children, ye shall not enter the Kingdom of God."

This man was more than peculiar, he was unique. In the field of prayer no prophet of old was ever held in greater reverence by his generation than Robert Sayers Sheffey. There are thousands of stories of remarkable answers to prayers that could be printed. The author has sifted these and given only those that are well substantiated in the book which many families in Southwestern Virginia and Southern West Virginia will want as well as many others who have gone out from this section.

                        Lewis W. Pierce
              District Supt. Methodist Church
              Tazewell, Virginia

Introduction

It has been generally agreed, and the wish often expressed, that some account of the character and labors of the Reverend Sayers Sheffey should be put into print. "Brother Sheffey" is the designation by which he was known. Soon after the father's death, his son, Edward S. Sheffey, prominent Methodist layman of Lynchburg, Virginia, indicated his purpose to write, or have written such a biography, but the plan was never carried out. It is probable that others would have taken the matter in hand at an earlier date but for the impression that such a volume was in preparation.

The public is indebted to Reverend Willard S. Barbery, whose ministry has been almost exclusively in the territory covered by Brother Sheffey's itineraries, for the service he has rendered in assembling the materials, interviewing those who knew and heard him, visiting the places where he preached and prayed, and preparing the chapters of this long awaited biography.

The book has come none too soon. Those who personally knew the unique man and felt the impact of his singular influence are rapidly passing, and with them would have passed also authentic testimony of the transactions here recorded. Oral testimony has necessarily been the author's chief reliance. Brother Sheffey was no writer, left no manuscripts, perhaps never in his life wrote a sermon, and only once or twice contributed an article to the newspaper. Letters written to friends are extant, usually lengthy and sometimes biographical in content, and have received careful attention by the author. Such materials as have been found have been given in the exact language in these pages, furnishing source records to those desiring to attempt further interpretation of this prophet of prayer.

Of the reliability of the things recorded there is no ground for question. Discrimination has been exercised in separating actual occurrence from rumor and tradition that invariably spring into currency where a figure such as Brother Sheffey too numerous to undervalue and too specific to fairly dispute, is involved in public discussion. Sane and balanced minds, unite in supporting these recitals, particularly the remarkable prayer answers that attended his travels covering a half century.

It is the author's purpose primarily to preserve these facts, rather than to philosophize about them. Where his opinion is given, however, it is unbiased and well-founded. The reader is left to draw such conclusions as may suit his inclination. Candid students of local church annals or of the the unexplored reaches of the prayer mystery should keep one or two things free from doubt, the actual occurrence of these incidents, the impression the man made wherever his visits were scheduled and the influence, remarkably vital, still in evidence where he lived and wrought many years ago.

This volume will be welcome by hundreds of families and their connections, in whose domestic circles its subject was entertained and offered his petitions, and will be read with profit by all who are interested in the factors entering into the evangelistic idealism characteristic of the upper Holston regions. Certainly the author will have the appreciation of the public at large for the considerable labor involved in this task undertaken and carried out while busy with his pastoral duties, and with no compensation except the consciousness of rendering a needed item of service.

                        E. E. Wiley
                        Trinity Methodist Chapel
                        Bluefield, West Virginia

The Author's Word

I have been asked why I became interested in writing a story of the life of Rev. Robert Sayers Sheffey. In the first place, I wanted to preserve to posterity the real character of this saint of God. In the second place, I have always been interested in knowing more about this personality than the mere traditions and stories told concerning this man who had such a tremendous hold upon the lives and the characters of people of sixty years ago. And, lastly, I saw in that face, when a mere boy, something that gripped my heart and soul, and I have had a deep desire to pass on to others through these written pages that something that stirred my being and made me want to be a better man. In these writings I have sought to give facts authenticated by persons who knew him in the flesh and whose lives were "made over" by this living dynamo of spiritual energy.

The facts, as set forth in these writings, have been gathered across many months of painstaking toil and effort. I would have failed but for the generous co-operation of numbers of friends who were in sympathy with my purposes. I especially want to thank Dr. E. E. Wiley, then pastor of Trinity Methodist Church, Bluefield, West Virginia, for his many kindnesses during the preparation of these pages, for the patience with which he listened to the reading of the manuscript and for the kind words of introduction. Also to Rev. Lewis W. Pierce, then district superintendent of the Tazewell district, for his assistance and the preface in this book. I want to thank Mr. Aurelius Vest, of White Gate, Va., for allowing me to use certain letters, etc., in his possession. The stories that are set forth in these pages came from friends stretched across the country. To all these, and to every one who has granted me any assistance I desire to express my heartfelt thanks and appreciation. The response to my efforts have been an hundred-fold, and I trust that the Spirit of the Great and Good God who directed the footsteps of Rev. Robert Sayers Sheffey may brood over each of you and bring you at last into the haven of rest where the soul of the old preacher has found rest.

W. S. Barbery
Bluefield, Virginia

A Courier of the Long Trail

Chapter I

Methodism Is Born

I think it was about five this morning that I opened my Testament on these words: 'There are given unto us exceeding great and precious promises, even that ye should be partakers of the divine nature.' (2 Peter 1:4). Just as I went out I opened it again on these words: 'Thou art not far from the kingdom of God.' In the afternoon I was asked to go to St. Paul's. The anthem was, 'Out of the deep have I called unto thee, O Lord: hear my voice.'

"In the evening I went very unwillingly to a society in Aldersgate Street, where one was reading Luther's preface to the Epistle to the Romans. About a quarter before nine, while he was describing the change which God works in the heart through faith in Christ, I felt my heart strangely warmed. I felt I did trust in Christ, Christ alone, for salvation; and an assurance was given me, that He had taken away my sins, even mine, and saved me from the law of sin and death.

"I began to pray with all my might for those who had in a more especial manner despitefully used me and persecuted me. I then testified openly to all there what I now felt first in my heart."

It was Wednesday, May 24, 1738, that John Wesley inscribed these words upon the pages of his "Journal." They tell the story of the great experience of a man who in the providence of God became the leader of one of the greatest religious bodies in the world. Today more than nine millions of people in every part of the world honor his name and are proud to bear the label of the Methodist church.

Wesley's experience worked a revolution in his life. It

has also worked a revolution in the world. And it will continue to work a revolution in every individual life, because it is through this experience that men come to know God and His Christ in the salvation of their souls. The amazing thing about it all may be seen in a revelation of what God can do with a single man who is willing to be guided by His Spirit. It is a thrilling illustration of the accomplishments of a lone man who dared to "carry the Cross" with the hope in his heart that he might "wear the crown." But the one thing that needs to be remembered is that Wesley had the great experience which makes the difference between a courageous man and a coward. And the crying need of the present century of Methodism is a valid experience of God. Wesley did not amount to very much as a religionist until after he had had the experience. But there was a revolutionary change in his life after that evening of May 24, 1738.

And writing about Methodists for Methodist enlightenment it might be well to record here what John Wesley calls the marks of a Methodist. His words might give us a better understanding of the character of the man in whose memory these pages are written. For certainly no man ever bore the marks of a Methodist with greater credit to himself and to the Christ whose cause he espoused than did Robert Sayers Sheffey, the subject of whom we write. Here are Wesley's own words:

"A Methodist is one who has the love of God shed abroad in his heart by the Holy Ghost given unto him: one who loves the Lord his God with all his heart, and soul, and mind, and strength. He rejoices evermore, prays without ceasing, and in everything gives thanks. His heart is full of love to all mankind, and is purified from envy, malice, wrath, and every unkind affection. His one desire, and the one desire of his life, is not to do his will, but the will of Him that sent him. He keeps all God's commandments, from the least to the greatest.

"He follows, not the customs of the world, for vice does not lose its nature through its becoming fashionable. He fares not sumptuously every day. He cannot lay up treasures upon earth: nor can he adorn himself with gold and costly apparel. He cannot speak evil of his neighbor any more than he can tell a lie. He cannot utter unkind or evil words. No corrupt communication ever comes out of his mouth. He does good unto all men; unto neighbors, strangers, friends and enemies. These are the principles and practices of our sect. These are the marks of a true Methodist. By these alone do Methodists desire to be distinguished from other men."

Methodists might well afford to memorize "the principles and practices of our sect" for these are days when principles and practices are being tried in the very crucible of fire. Christian people are being called to live under greater pressure at this hour than at any other period of our history save those first days of the Christian fathers. But men and women of the Christian faith have seen the light of the dawning of a new day of hope. The fires of Methodism are being re-kindled and more than nine millions of them have joined together in singing that old Methodist hymn of Charles Wesley written as he meditated upon "the great experience" as it came to him:

> "O for a thousand tongues to sing
> My great Redeemer's praise,
> The glory of my God and King,
> The triumphs of His grace!
> "My gracious Master and my God
> Assist me to proclaim,
> To spread through all the earth abroad
> The honors of Thy name.
> "Jesus! the Name that charms our fears,
> That bids our sorrows cease,
> 'Tis music in the sinner's ears,
> 'Tis life, and health, and peace.
> "He breaks the power of cancelled sin,
> He sets the prisoner free;
> His blood can make the foulest clean;
> His blood availed for me."

Heroes of the Cross are to the manner born, first of the flesh and then of the Spirit. But after the second birth and their new creation, their whole lives become the property of their new Master and fleshly desires and ambitions are gone forever. The founder of Methodism is a thrilling example of that religious fervor which completely possessed and controlled that man who had been given a God-bent mission.

Frank S. Mead, the author of that most interesting book, "The March of Eleven Men," says of Wesley: "He literally leaped into the saddle. He bought a horse, stuffed his saddlebags with books, and rode grimly out to joust with England's evil. He rode forty-five hundred miles a year, two hundred and fifty thousand miles in all before he finally stepped down out of the saddle. He was up at four in the morning, he had preached by five, by seven he was off down the road to his second preaching point, reading and studying as he rode. He preached from two to five sermons a day for over fifty years, better than forty-two thousand in all. He rode in the rain and winter winds, he swam his horse across swollen angry rivers, he traveled roads infested with highwaymen and murderers, he took his life in his hands a hundred times as he faced belligerent, excited mobs. And this man never weighed more than one hundred and twenty pounds in his life! He rode and preached in the wreck-strewn wake of the Industrial Revolution and made his way into the heart of England. He has been called a vitalized shuttle-cock, weaving the destiny of England.

"Only a few came to hear him at first. Then hundreds. Then thousands and tens of thousands. His audiences spread out over the fields and hillsides like great hungry flocks of sheep. He preached, at seventy years of age, to twenty and thirty thousand people a day. Dirty-faced miners from the Cornwall mines; half-dead laborers from the factory and the mill; owners of mills and managers of factories, responsible for such conditions and mildly curious about his preaching, rubbed shoulders with their victims, the human wrecks who were perishing for the lack of it. To all of them he preached, 'Repent ye, for . . .' and 'Now is the day of salvation.' He drove into the hearts of the despondent masses the exhilarating thought that in them, oppressed and broken as they were, were divine possibilities; they were the children of God, loved by Him though oppressed by men; they were sinners, to be sure, but sinners who might be saved by a single act of faith in Christ. He drew thousands of those beaten ones to their knees in a new devotion to righteousness; he swept other thousands of the higher classes to their knees side by side with the lowly."

The spirit has given to the world one of its most dominant religious faiths. It has also given to the world many of its most scintillating personalities.

Methodism was born out of the experience of John Wesley who had felt his heart "strangely warmed." From that Aldersgate Street experience he stepped out into a new world with a newborn purpose in his heart and soul. Two hundred years have passed into the lap of the eternities, but the spirit of John Wesley rides on, and will continue to ride until time has been finished and eternity begun.

In less than fifty years after its birth Methodism had crossed the Atlantic Ocean and planted itself in the homes of the pioneers who had established themselves in a new world. It came not with a noisy fanfare of trumpets. It never sought to display itself. It came because there was a need for the kind of a gospel it endeavored to preach and live. It came because it had in it the qualities and the elements that make for real hardness of character and these were the essential requirements of life in a new world.

Methodism has always been a pioneering religion. It has never sought the easy places. Wherever there were men and women lost in the pitfalls of sin it sought to bring to them the glorious light and liberty of the Christian gospel. In the homes of the pioneers, with the crude light of the pine torch, it set up its altar and began to preach. Into the forests, where the timber-men were hewing the logs for their cabins, it came with its message of love and redemption. In the lumbering camps, where men cursed and raved at their teams, its messenger climbed on to the stump of a fallen monarch of the forest and delivered his story of salvation and passed on his way. It has stood at the mouth of the coal-pit where the miners have passed out of the light of day into the darkness of night to dig the "black diamonds" with which to warm the bodies of men and women and little children. It has spoken out of the freight car which has become the meeting-house of the humble folk.

Methodism has dared to do these things because it had a message. That message had been made to live in the hearts of humble souls and it could not be silenced. It must be made to live in the hearts of others. And on down through the years men and women have marched with the fervor and the zeal of the eleven men who companied with Jesus.

In the history of the human race, one great road stands out above all other roads. It is the road to Damascus. Victor Hugo, in his "Shakespeare," says, "The road to Damascus shall be forever the route of great minds. It shall also be the route of nations." Because men and women have dared to travel in this road, light has broken upon all the highways of the world, and peace has come to multiplied millions of souls throughout the earth.

The same light that fell athwart the pathway of Saul of Tarsus in the long ago has been the light that has led the Methodist church on to its deserved achievements. The same Spirit has guided its course across the oceans, and the swollen streams, and over the mountains, and into the hollows where men and women needed God.

It was about one hundred and fifty years ago that Methodism made its advent into this area now known as the Tazewell district and contiguous territory of the Holston conference, one of the great conferences of all Methodism. The first citizens had scarcely had time enough to build their cabins before they were visited by a Methodist preacher. In these cabins he preached and held his revivals. The threat of the redskins, the brewing of the storm, swollen streams did not deter him. He had a message and he must deliver it.

E. Merton Coulter in his life of William G. Brownlow, "The Fighting Parson of the Southern Highlands," says: "Carrying religion to the frontier was beset with almost as many dangers and inconveniences as dogged the steps of the Crusaders in the Holy Lands. The Methodist circuit-rider was in the forefront; the Baptist itinerant was not far behind; the Presbyterians, while generally early on the field, enjoyed more security back of the lines."

The Methodist circuit-rider was God's evangel. He did not seek security. He wanted to be in the forefront. He had sufficient faith in God to keep his soul steady as he journeyed on his way. Like Abraham of old, "he went out, not knowing whither he went." He was "a hard rider, a hard preacher, and a hard liver." These were his daily experiences. Speaking of the Methodist itineracy in those days, Bishop Wm. W. Wightman, in his "Life of William Capers, D. D.," said, "It had no ruffles or lawn sleeves that it cared to soil, no lovelocks that it feared to disorder, no buckles it was loath to tarnish. It lodged roughly, and it fared scantily. It tramped up muddy ridges, it swam or forded rivers to the waist; it slept on leaves or raw deer-skin, and pillowed its head on saddle-bags; it bivouacked among wolves or Indians; now it suffered from ticks or mosquitos—it was attacked by dogs, it was hooted, and it was pelted—but it throve."

Quoting Coulter again, "He threaded his way through the wilderness with a Bible in one hand and a sword in the other. He might have had imperfect notions of the universe outside of the Southern Appalachians, but he was seriously going about the task which he knew it was his duty to perform. His language was fiery and direct, for he knew he had a great issue to settle every time he preached. He had the conviction that there were souls in his audience which if not saved then would go down to eternal damnation before he should return."

Bishop Francis Asbury, "the Prophet of the Long Road," came to America in the year 1784. In less than a decade the circuit-rider came with his saddle-bags, Bible, and a few choice books. These were his sole possessions save his unshaken faith in God, and Jesus Christ, and the Holy Spirit. But there burned within his soul an unquieted passion for the souls of men. It was this passion that drove him ever onward into the trackless forests with the message of an undying love for lost souls.

It has been said of Methodism that she has always possessed a passion for evangelism. From the days of the Wesleys she has gone on her way carrying the blood-stained banner of the Son of God as its emblem. She has never known retreat. Her battle song has been "Onward, Christian Soldier." She has asked no quarter. With her standard—the Cross of Christ, the emblem of the Crusaders—she has always marched in the forefront of human progress and human achievement.

I see her as she plows her way through the trackless forests of the New World. There are obstacles that are apparently insurmountable, but ever onward she goes. "There are wildernesses that are untrodden and pathless; there are forests which are the abode of savages and wild beasts; there are no places of friendly shelter for the itinerant; there are no expectant eyes watching for their coming; there was no board of missions to give them assurance of support. Through the wild solitude they journeyed, not to seek wealth nor ease, but to endure hardship, toil, and peril for the sake of Christ and lost souls."

About the year 1856, Rev. William Henry Milburn, D. D., wrote a lecture on "The Pioneer Preacher, or Rifle, Axe, and Saddle-Bags," in which he portrays the early life of the pioneer Methodist preacher. His picture is so realistic that we herewith reproduce it so that the readers of this book may understand something of the hardships of those men who have made possible the Methodist church in this hill country. We quote as follows:

"You may see him riding up some evening to the door of a cabin, where he is to lodge, and as it is a pretty fair specimen of the houses in the country, you may desire a description of it. The cabin is twelve by fourteen feet, and one story high. The spaces between the logs are chinked and then daubed with mud for plaster. The interior consists of one room, one end of which is occupied by a fireplace. In this one room are to sleep the man, his wife, the fifteen or twenty children bestowed upon them by Providence—for Providence is bountiful in this matter upon the border—and as the woods are full of 'varmints,' hens and chickens must be brought in for safe-keeping, and as the dogs constitute an important portion of every hunter's family, they also take pot-luck with the rest. Fastened to a tree near the door is a clap-board, upon which is traced, in characters of Charcoal, a sentence to the following effect—which you may read if you are keen at deciphering hieroglyphics: 'Akomidation fur man and Beast.'

"In this one room the family are to perform their manifold household offices. Here their sleeping, cooking, eating, washing, preaching and hearing are to be performed. Amid the driving storms of winter, it is of course impossible for our youthful theologian to transform an old log or the shadow of a tree into a study; his book must therefore be carried into the house, where he is surrounded by a motley group. Of course a hunter never swears in bad weather; the lady of the house never scolds; children of all ages never quarrel and raise a row; dogs never bark and fight, nevertheless, you may imagine that if our student is able to confine his attention to the page, deriving mental nutriment from the lettered line, he must possess not a little power of concentration and abstraction. He may obtain permission of his host to pursue his studies after the rest of the family have retired. Lighting a pine knot, he sticks it up in one corner of the huge fire-place, lays himself down on the flat of his stomach in the ashes, glowing with transport over 'the thoughts that breathe and the words that burn.' These are what poets call 'the midnight oil,' and 'cloisters pale.' Not a few men have I known who acquired the mastery of the Latin and Greek Tongue, and much valuable and curious lore in such "grottoes and caves' as these.

"Possibly there may be another apartment in the cabin. If so, it is denominated the 'prophet's chamber.' You gain access to it by a rickety step-ladder in one corner of the cabin. Toiling up this steep ascent you reach a loft, formed by laying loose clap-boards on the rafters. With dubious tread and careful steps, you pick your way across the floor. I have said the clap-boards are loose, and if you are not cautious, one end will fly up and the other down, in company with which latter you shall be precipitated upon the sleepers below. Having reached the opposite end of the loft, the prophet's bed is discovered. It is a bear-skin, a buffalo-skin, or a tick filled with shucks. Having laid him on his couch, our prophet, if he be thoughtfully inclined, can study Astronomy from his resting-place, through the rifts in the roof; and when it rains or snows, he has the benefit of the hydropathic treatment, without fee or prescription.

"He must ford or swim mountain torrents as they boil and rush along their downward channels, in cold weather as in warm. Often he emerged from the wintry streams, his garments glittering in the clear, cold sunlight, as if they had been of burnished steel-armor, chill as the touch of death. During that twelve-months, in the midst of such scenes, he traveled on foot and horseback four thousand miles, preached four hundred times; and found on casting up the receipts, yarn socks, woolen vests, cotton shirts, and a little silver change, that his salary amounted to twelve dollars and ten cents."

It was such a pleasure as this that was presented to the eyes of Jeremiah Lambert, said to have been the first Methodist preacher appointed to the work west of the Allegheny mountains. Lambert may be considered as the first missionary of American Methodism. When he first came to the Holston Circuit, embracing eastern Tennessee and a large part of South-western Virginia, it was a mission field of undetermined area.

Lambert's coming was about the year 1783-84. The country was sparsely settled, provisions were scarce, the Indians troublesome, his hardships and sufferings terrible, no accomodations for traveling, lodging, or anything else. And without hope of any earthly reward, and often without food and shelter, he made his way as best he could in the name and for the sake of Him who said, "Lo, I am with you alway, even unto the end of the world."

One of the first of these early pioneers of the Cross was the Rev. John Kobler, sent to the New River Circuit in the year 1794. His preaching places were in the homes of the people throughout the area he traversed. He preached in a home near the site of the present town of Tazewell. This was really the beginning of Methodism in the heart of what is now known as the great Tazewell district of the Methodist church, in the Holston Conference. He was instrumental in the establishment of a church on a plat of ground donated by Thomas Peery. This is believed to have been the first church of any denomination in Tazewell county. As a result of his preaching on one of his first visits to this section ten white persons and two colored persons were converted and a congregation formed.

Another early preacher in this section was the Rev. Jacob Young who met his congregations in the homes of the pioneers along the Clinch and Bluestone Rivers. He remained only one year. He was a very able man and hailed from the state of Pennsylvania. Bishop Asbury sent him to the work in 1804 with the admonition, "Pray as often as you eat." That admonition could not afford to be ignored for dangers were many, enemies were countless, and unbeaten paths were the haunts of savages.

Young had a great deal of trouble in organizing a circuit until he was able to dispel the feeling of the people that he was a Baptist. On one occasion, as darkness was fast approaching, he spied a cabin in the midst of the forest. He approached and asked the woman in the door-way whether he might spend the night. She was on the point of turning him away as a roving Baptist. He explained that he was a Methodist. And thereupon she exclaimed, "La, me! has a Methodist preacher come at last? Yes, brother, you shall stay all night."

The Pulaski County Centennial edition of the Southwest Times, published at Pulaski, Virginia, on Sunday, August 13, 1939, carried a very interesting article relative to the founding of the Methodist church in Southwest Virginia. The article was written by Mrs. R. H. Wooling. That portion which we are using says:

"The first circuit in this country was 'America,' rather a large one. Robert Williams was the first Methodist to marry on Virginia soil, formed the first society, printed the first Methodist book, first to die, first of the heroes to pass into the city of God.

"The first Methodist society in Pulaski county was organized at Page's meeting house or near there in the year 1773. It was Montgomery county then. Page's meeting house was a log church and was a preaching place for nearly a century. It was supplanted by a neat frame church during the ministry of Dr. W. H. Price. This church was built about one-fourth of a mile north of the New River bridge on the N. & W. Ry. It was named Morgan's chapel in honor of Edward Morgan who was an Englishman by birth and who was ordained by John Wesley. He was a member of the first class ever formed in the neighborhood called the 'Irish Settlement,' in Giles county. He was a very useful local preacher in the early days of this church.

"Our first Methodist bishop, Asbury, visited this

'meeting house,' the Morgan's chapel, during his itineraries."

The Methodist churches of this part of the Holston country have had a long and glorious history. About her altars cluster many precious memories. Memories that are rich and rare. And many choice souls, born at those altars, are the heritage of a great people.

Some sixty odd years ago there stood an old camp-ground site about six miles west of what is now the thriving city of Bluefield, Virginia. This is said to have been one of the largest camp-grounds for Methodist people in all the Holston area in its great day. It was known as the Charles' Chapel, named in honor of Rev. James Charles, who lived near what is now called Witten's Mill, a flag-station on the Norfolk & Western railway between Bluefield and Norton. This man is believed to have been one of the first local preachers in the Methodist itineracy, in all this country.

A few years ago, while I was the pastor of the Graham Circuit I was out visiting in the neighborhood of the Witten's Mill church. I had pointed out to me an old and abandoned cemetery on a hillside not so far removed from what is now the Smoot home, once the home of the Charles family. With considerable difficulty I made my way to the spot and there I found the grave of this old "soldier of the Cross." The grave-stone which marked the spot where the sacred dust of this saint of olden days rests had been broken from its pedestal, and the passing years, with the fury of the storm, had almost destroyed the legibility of the inscription on the stone. The inscription read: "Here lies the remains of Rev. James Charles, a local preacher in the Methodist Episcopal Church, South. Ordained a deacon by Bishop Asbury in 1808; ordained an elder by Bishop McKendree in 1811." This stone was evidently erected after the separation of the church. No living person in that community seemed to know anything about who placed the stone at the head of the grave where some cattle were grazing that day as I searched for the stone which had been broken off at the base and covered over with dirt and red clayey soil.

The history of this man's ministry has been lost sight of in the mists and fogs of the passing years. But it is very probable, reckoning from the years of his active ministry, that he had more to do with the establishment of Methodism in the hill-country of Tazewell county and adjacent territory than any other man. The Old Charles' Chapel meeting-house, near where Ebenezer church (on Graham Circuit) now stands, was named in his honor. It is likely that he traveled many miles on horseback to attend some session of the Holston Conference to have conferred upon him the honors of a deacon's and elder's orders. Those were days when the circuit riders had to travel hundreds of miles to attend the sessions of the Conference. They were away from their homes for weeks at a time while their families remained at home to care for themselves.

One day I visited in the home of Mr. James H. Summers, a few miles west of Bluefield, Virginia, and we discussed the history of the old Charles' Chapel church. Among some old records in Mr. Summers' possession I found the names of the original class of worshippers. The names as recorded were: Joseph A. Moore, Martha Moore, Christina Moore, Howard Bane, Mattie Bane, John Harry, Randall Holbrook, Polly Holbrook, Charles F. Tiffany, Wm. R. Bane, Nancy Bane, Wm. K. Shannon, Polly Shannon, Martha P. Moore, Caroline E. Harry, Nancy Flummer, and George Reynolds. There were seventeen persons included among the first members of this Methodist church in the eastern end of Tazewell county. Their descendants are to be found in almost every Protestant church in this whole area adjacent to Tazewell county and the city of Bluefield. And there are many in the southern parts of West Virginia.

Joseph A. Moore and Christian Moore were the grandparents of Frank K. Karr who now resides in Wright's Valley, near Bailey Methodist church, Tazewell county; Howard Bane and Mattie Bane were the grandparents of Mr. Summers, mentioned above; Randall Holbrook and Polly Holbrook were the parents of "Uncle Jimmie" Holbrook, father of Rev. Z. D. Holbrook, for a half century or more a useful member of the Holston Conference. Charles F. Tiffany was the grandfather of Dr. Wade St. Clair and Dr. Charles St. Clair, eminent physicians of Bluefield, W. Va.; also John and Alex. St. Clair of

Bluefield, Va.; Wm. R. Bane and Nancy Bane were the parents of Mrs. D. H. Carr, Mrs. W. W. Hicks, and Mrs. Will Summers: Wm. K. Shannon and Polly Shannon were the grandparents of the late Wm. Shannon, a large landholder on Bluestone; Martha P. Moore has prominent descendants residing in the Wright's Valley section of Tazewell county. She was a member of the Moore family of Abb's Valley history; Nancy Flummer was the grandmother of Mrs. H. J. Harvey who lived on Bluestone for many years. "Uncle Jimmie" Holbrook, Wm. K. Shannon and George A. Reynolds were local preachers in the Methodist church. In the Wm. Bane family were three well known Methodist preachers, the Rev. Daniel H. Carr, Rev. W. W. Hicks, and Rev. George W. Summers.

The Charles' Chapel church, for many years known as the Bluestone Camp-Ground, was located on the "brow of the hill" near the home of Mr. Wm. Bane, a descendant of the Bane family mentioned in the church roll, close by the highway between the towns of Bluefield, Virginia, and Tazewell, Virginia.

It has been men like some of those mentioned above who have made possible the great Methodist church as we know it today. They had but few, if any, programs. Their task was to preach the Word. They were laying the foundation stones. And they laid them well and deep. They were men of great courage and great faith. Like shadows, their memories linger in almost every community of the great Southwestern portion of Virginia and even over into adjacent states. Many of them have been outstanding Christian characters, and today "their works do follow them." Through years of adversity they toiled for a mere pittance. In many instances it was not enough to keep the wolves away from their doors, but they pressed ahead. Their eyes were always on the Cross. Their pathways have been beset with obstacles of every known character and type, but they have not lived and labored in vain. Men and women by the thousands rise up to bless the memory of their names and to exalt the Christ for whom they lived and died.

Most of them were unlearned, but earthly wisdom had been laid aside for the wisdom of God. In that circle they moved and God supplied their needs for the day and hour in which they lived. Some of them were eccentric and possessed many peculiarities, but God can turn the foolishness of man into ways of wisdom to defeat the schemes of the devil.

Chapter II
Robert Sayers Sheffey

"Great may he be who can command
And rule with just and tender sway;
Yet is diviner wisdom taught
Better by him who can obey.
Blessed are they who die for God
And earn the martyr's crown of light;
Yet he who lives for God may be
A greater conqueror in His sight."
—Adelaide Proctor

One of the most interesting characters of the Christian ministry ever seen in this hill-country was Robert Sayers Sheffey, born in the little community of Ivanhoe, Wythe county, Virginia, on July 4, 1820. He came of pioneer parents, settlers in one of the most beautiful sections of Southwest Virginia. His family has long been prominent in affairs of state, and his ancestors and descendants are among the most noteworthy in the entire Southwestern portion of Virginia. They have stood for the finest and the best in all that pertains to the citizenship of this proud old "Mother of States."

The name of "Uncle Bob" Sheffey is known in almost every home, village, town, and city of Southwestern Virginia, Southern West Virginia and East Tennessee. For more than a half-century men and women have told one story after another of the interesting experiences of this eccentric itinerant Methodist preacher. The homes where he used to stop in many instances retain interesting relics of his visits. It may be just a chair in which he used to sit. It may be a picture that he has drawn upon some rock, or a knot, or a frog stool. He seems to have had the soul of an artist, and oftentimes in his visits among his friends he would give expression in a living way to the artistic bent of his soul. As he rode along the highways, or the trails, he would find time to stop and pray and write upon a rock some scriptural truth or admonition.

A connected history of the Sheffey family at this late

day has been rather difficult to obtain owing to the fact that the minds of men grow dim with the passing of the years. Only the briefest records are obtainable and these after months of pain-taking research have been made in many parts of the country. Most of the older members of the family have died and only a few of the grandchildren of Robert Sayers Sheffey are now living. These know but brief facts about the progenitors of this man who was perhaps known by more people in his active days throughout the Southwestern section of Virginia and Southern West Virginia than any other figure who moved across its frontiers.

Many stories of the Sheffey family have been related during the past one hundred and fifty years, but only brief references have been made to their ancestry. Hon. David E. Johnson, in 1905 wrote a history of the Middle New River settlements and contiguous territory. He writes several interesting stories about Robert Sayers Sheffey, some of which are recited herein, but he gives no history of the family. Rev. J. Wesley Smith, D. D., in 1902, wrote a story of the mountaineers in which he gives quite a number of Sheffey's experiences as an itinerant preacher. Here again, there are no facts concerning the Sheffey family. He records that Robert Sayers Sheffey "was born of respected and well-to-do parents, and was one of several children. Two or three of his brothers were lawyers and attained prominence in their profession, leaders at the bar and on the bench."

As important as heritage may be, as splendid as it is to have good blood in one's veins, Sheffey's character did not depend upon the background of his life. He built his own character upon the foundation stones of faith in God and daily contacts with the Holy Spirit which is the Guide of every life that happens to be God-centered. Quoting Smith: "If every man is the architect of his own fortune, then may we say that Sheffey with his own hand carved for himself a monument as enduring as the chiseled granite, the memory of whose life will linger long after the names of stars of seeming greater magnitude have been forgotten. His unbounded enthusiasm and zeal in life's one purpose and aim to him—to see souls made better and to glorify God

—never faltered or waned. Not in the mountains of Virginia, nor on their rock ribs of granite base, but in the hearts and homes of the people, graven with memory's pen on immortal tablets, is that unassuming, unpretending, humble name of Bob Sheffey, the man of God."

A few years ago Dr. Goodridge A. Wilson, former pastor of the Presbyterian Royal Oak Church in Marion, Virginia, published in his "Southwest Corner," appearing in the Roanoke Times each Sunday, an interesting story of the Sheffey family. A member of the family gave this article to us and much of it is here reproduced:

"The Sheffey family started in Virginia with two brothers of German descent, Daniel and Henry L. Sheffey, who came into this State from Maryland. Daniel, the older, stopped in Wythe county, later removing to Staunton, where he died in 1830. Henry went to Abingdon, where he married Miss Margaret White, sister of James White, one of the wealthiest of Southwest Virginia's early business men. They were men of intellectual force, genuine, genial and companionable, gifted conversationalists, witty, and quick at repartee. They had little or no money, and made their living as they went along by whatever means came to hand."

Howe's "History of Virginia" says: "Daniel Sheffey was born at Frederick, Maryland, 1770, and was bred a shoemaker in his father's shop. His education was inconsiderable, but possessing an ardent desire for knowledge he passed his leisure time in reading. Arrived at manhood he traveled on foot, with his 'kit' on his back to Winchester. Thence he walked through the Valley of Virginia, stopping at villages on his route and earning money by his trade to pay his expenses, until he arrived at Abbeville, Wythe county. He was a stranger, friendless and destitute, and here he commenced his trade once more. The novelty and originality of his character, and the flashes of genius which enlivened his conversation often compelled his new-tried friends to look on the eccentric youth with wonder. Becoming popular he was received into the office of Alexander Smythe, Esq., and after being admitted to the bar of Wythe county was employed in the most important suits. After some years he settled in Staunton and obtained a lucrative practice. He often represented Augusta in the House of Delegates. In 1811 Mr. Sheffey was elected to Congress and by sheer ability obtained marked recognition in that august body. He was one of the few congressmen who got the better of John Randolph of Roanoke in repartee. Randolph once remarked, in commenting on a speech by Mr. Sheffey, that 'the shoemaker ought not to go beyond his last.' Sheffey quickly retorted: 'If the gentleman had ever been on the bench, he never would have left it.' From his home in Staunton he often traveled through Southwest Virginia on legal business, where he was very popular, especially with the numerous German element with whom he conversed in their mother tongue.

"Henry L. Sheffey, the younger brother, after his marriage to Margaret White, moved to a farm on Cripple Creek in Wythe county. His wife died there, leaving him with five little boys, the oldest ten years of age and the youngest two. Two years later he died, and the boys were taken by relatives. Their names were: Daniel, James White, Hugh, Lawrence and Robert Sayers. Daniel and Hugh were taken by their uncle Daniel in Staunton; the other three went to live with their mother's folks in Abingdon.

"Daniel Sheffey, Jr., was a most promising lad. When about twelve years of age he became totally blind from over-study. He lived to be about sixty years old, traveling frequently on horseback from Staunton to Washington county, with his violin as his companion and Randal, a negro servant, to care for him. He was welcomed everywhere, not only because of his musical ability, but also because he was called 'good company.' Few men were more companionable and better informed. His last years were spent on what is now known as the Peters' farm, near Emory. He lived, and died, in the old log house still standing on the road between Emory and Glad Spring.

"James White Sheffey, the second of the five orphaned sons of Henry L. and Margaret White Sheffey, eight years old when his mother died, came to the young county seat village of Marion in 1835 as a young lawyer, bringing with him his bride, the former Miss Ellen Fairman Preston, the daughter of Colonel John Preston of Walnut Grove, Washington county. He was a great lawyer, a good farmer, and shrewd far-seeing man of business. He became, perhaps, the largest land owner in Southwest Virginia. He was a member of the Secession Convention of Virginia in 1861. In 1876 while attending the sessions of the legislature as a delegate from Smyth county, he was stricken with illness in Richmond and died in June of that year, sixty-three years old.

"James White Sheffey was a handsome man of distinguished and dignified bearing, very meticulous as to his dress. He is said to have been down-right provoked at times with his brother Bob for coming in shabbily garbed after having given away his good clothes to some poor fellow whom 'Uncle Robert' thought needed them worse than he did.

"James White Sheffey had six daughters and one son who grew to maturity. His son and four daughters married and lived in Marion, rearing their families there, that is all who had families. His son, Judge John Preston Sheffey, spent his life in Marion and reared there his family of five daughters and two sons. Two of his daughters, Mrs. B. F. Buchanan and Mrs. E. M. Copenhaver, are living in Marion now."—(End quote).

A few years ago there came from the press a book bearing the title, "Addresses of Famous Southwest Virginians," compiled by Hon. C. Bascon Slemp, former member of the Congress from the Ninth district of Virginia, in which may be found a speech made by the Hon. Daniel Sheffey, Congressman, before the House of Representatives on the subject of "Opposition to the War of 1812."

The Marion, (Virginia), Democrat of May, 1928, carried an abridged article written by Judge John Preston Sheffey which gave a brief history of the Sheffey family. It is reprinted herein as it is a true sketch of the background of this illustrious family which had a prominent part in the history of Southwestern Virginia. It follows:

"In the latter part of the eighteenth century, two brothers of Dutch descent removed from Maryland into Virginia. They were men of intellectual ability, culture and refinement. The oldest was Daniel Sheffey, who came as far as Wythe county. He was a stranger, friendless and destitute. For a while he cobbled shoes to gain a means of livelihood. He possessed an ardent desire for knowledge, read all the books he could find, and was particularly fond of astronomical and mathematical studies. He turned his attention to law, and was received into the office of Alexander Smyth, for whom Smyth county was named. He was admitted to the bar of Wythe county, and was employed in important suits. After some years, he settled at Staunton and became a lawyer of distinction. He traveled in the practice of his profession through the Valley of Virginia, the New River and Holston Valley to the Virginia border. Being able to converse with the Dutch and German people of these valleys in their native languages marked him as one of them and added greatly to his popularity. Though a master of pure English he spoke with a decided brogue. He was also popular with the Scotch-Irish who had settled in these valleys for there is nothing more admired by the people of that strain than mental ability, wit and industry. So for a number of years he was sent to the House of Representatives from the Augusta district. While in Congress he became still more distinguished, especially for his power in debate, and for the flashes of genius which enlivened his speeches. He died in Augusta county in 1830.

"The other brother was Henry L. Sheffey who came out to Southwest Virginia and located in Washington county. At Abingdon he married Margaret White, a sister of Col. James White, who was a man of extraordinary ability and of great wealth for his day. Henry Sheffey and his wife moved to Wythe country and settled on a farm on Cripple Creek. Here he, in farming and superintending his servants, and she in household cares and the management of their children, spent the years of their married life. Five sons were born to them, Daniel, Jr., the eldest less than eleven years old when his mother died, and Robert Sayers Sheffey, the youngest, about two years old. The other sons were James White, Hugh and Lawrence. Henry Sheffey died two years after the death of his wife. The boys, Daniel and Hugh, were taken by their uncle to Staunton and by his help and means from their father's estate were reared and educated. When about twenty-one years of age Daniel became totally blind, the result of laborious study. He lived to be about 60 years old, traveling frequently on horseback from Staunton to Washington county with his violin as his companion and Randall, a negro attendant, to care for him. He was welcomed everywhere, not only because of his musical abilities, but because he was what is called 'good company.' Wherever he went he had his relatives and friends read to him historical and classic works, and the news of the day, so that few men were more companionable and better informed. He spent the last few years of his life on a farm belonging to his brother, James, near Emory and Henry College. Notwithstanding the handicap of blindness, he managed this large estate satisfactorily. He died at Emory and his grave is near there in the college cemetery.

"James White Sheffey, the second son of Henry and Margaret Sheffey, was born on the 15th of March, 1813, and was eight years old when his mother died. He and his brother, Lawrence, were taken to Abingdon by their maternal uncle, Col. James White, and made their home with him. James White Sheffey was educated in the school at Abingdon under the tutelage of Mr. David Speaker, and Mr. Bailey, a school which was celebrated in its day. In this school such boys as William C., John S., and Thomas L. Preston, Benjamin Rush Floyd, John Buchanan Floyd, Beverly, Charles, and John W. Johnston, Connally Trigg, John and Joseph T. Campbell and many such men were started on their careers of distinction. In such a school, and the debating society connected with it, James W. Sheffey was thrown into constant association with young men whose subsequent success attests the brightness of their intellects and their power of application. Under the influence of such environment, it is not strange that he should have acquired the graces of oratory, the power of concentration, the desire for knowledge, and the ambition for success. He read law under distinguished lawyers at Abingdon and at twenty-one years of age was admitted to the bar. His uncle, James White, soon entrusted him with important business connected with the Salt Works and Lead Mines in which Col. White had large interests. He went early in important cases to the court of appeals at Lewisburg, and his efforts were crowned with remarkable success. On the ninth of September, 1835, he was married to Ellen Fairman Preston, a daughter of Col. John Preston and Margaret Preston of Walnut Grove, Washington County. The young couple made their home in Marion, moving to that town shortly after their marriage. Eleven children were born to them, four of them dying in infancy.

"James W. Sheffey was eminently successful as a lawyer and farmer, investing his earnings principally in real estate. He associated his son, John Preston, as his partner in the practice of law in September, 1859, and this partnership, although interrupted by the absence of the son in the Confederate service, during the war, was never dissolved but by the death of the senior partner in June, 1876. James W. Sheffey was never very desirous of political preferment, but was sometimes nominated and compelled to run. In 1861 he was elected to the Secession Convention, though it was well known that he doubted the wisdom of secession, and hoped that Virginia could work out some other plan in those troublous times. The convention was composed of able statesmen, and many of them shared Mr. Sheffey's views on the policy of secession. On the third day of the convention, President Lincoln demanded from Virginia her quota of troops to fight against her sister Southern States which had seceded. This crystallized the sentiment in favor of secession, and on the seventeenth day of April, 1861, James W. Sheffey became one of the signers of the Ordinance by which Virginia seceded from the union.

"When the war was over, Wm. G. Brownlow whose son Mr. Sheffey had successfully defended in law suits, became active in securing his early pardon which was extended to him by President Johnson. In this matter he was more fortunate than Robert E. Lee whose application for pardon was never granted, and who died a disfranchised man. During the war, Mr. Sheffey was commissioned captain of the Home Guards which saw some service in guarding the bridges and tracks of the Virginia and Tennessee railroad. Upon one occasion he and his company captured a body of raiders who were traveling through the mountains. They were seen in Tazewell county and a message was sent to Mr. Sheffey that they were traveling on foot by compass and that the course would bring them out of the mountain at a certain point where he should intercept them. He speedily moved his company to the point stated, disposed them in heavy skirmish line across the course and advanced to meet the invaders. They had stopped at a mountain stream to rest and bathe their worn-out feet. A pursuing party from Tazewell came up and helped capture the raiders. After one volley, they surrendered and Mr. Sheffey and his troops brought the captured men to Marion whence they were sent the next day to the prison at Richmond. During the war Mr. Sheffey did everything in his power to advance the Southern cause. His doors were open with unstinted hospitality to the Southern soldiers, and he and his wife made every possible sacrifice to aid the Southern cause. When the war was ended, his lands lay in desolation—the fences were burned or decayed, the horses and cattle gone, there was not even seed for the sowing of a new crop. He had to begin anew. He brought to this task the indomitable spirit of the South—and in a few years, for fortune smiled upon him—there were again fields of grain, ripening for the harvest, and grazing lands dotted with flocks and herds. His profession, too, became profitable, and his reputation as a great lawyer was established. He chafed under the restraints of the reconstruction period and submitted with ill grace to the police regulations of the Federal soldiers who occupied his property and governed his town.

"In 1875 he was elected a member of the House of Delegates. At the session of 1876 he became ill in Richmond and his death occurred in June of that year at the early age of sixty-three. Among the books in his office were a dozen or more great volumes bound in calf-skin or cardboard. On the fly-leaf of each was written 'Copied from a book lent to me by Judge Estill.' These books painstakingly inscribed in long hand, on heavy foolscap paper were the nucleus of his law library. What patience and industry and ambition the young lawyer brought to the copying of all this mass of words, these thousands of pages! It is well that he achieved success—and better still that he deserved it.

"The other sons of Henry and Margaret Sheffey became distinguished in their chosen fields of activity.

Lawrence settled in Huntsville, Alabama, and became a physician of distinction. Hugh was the only one of the family who received anything like a complete college education. He was sent by his uncle Daniel to Yale where he was well equipped for the struggles of life. He became a noted lawyer and jurist. He was a member of the Convention of 1850-51 which passed the 'manhood' suffrage law. Before that convention only land owners could vote in Virginia. His home was in Staunton and he represented Augusta county during eleven terms in the legislature. For many years he was judge of the court of his district. He was a man of intellectual ability, high ideals and blameless life. Robert Sayers, the fifth son of Henry and Margaret Sheffey, became a Methodist preacher, distinguished for his unfaltering faith and power in prayer. He was not a man of books, but one book he loved, the Book of Books, which was a lamp unto his feet and a light unto his path. He was a prophet that was not without honor in his own country, and his memory still lives in the hearts and homes of the people of the mountains with whom he spent his life. He preached a plain gospel for a plain people, giving his life in loving ministry to the poor and lowly. Of the five Sheffey brothers, surely none better served his generation than the mountain preacher, known as Brother Bob Sheffey."

Sheffey's father, Henry L. Sheffey, lived on a small farm in Wythe county, for many years known as the Abram Painter place, in the small community of Ivanhoe. This community was then a small neighborhood of farmers. Later it became a bustling community where an iron furnace of the Virginia Iron Coal & Coke Company operated for several years. The plant has long since been dismantled and former evidences of the prosperity of the community have vanished. But few people living in the community are aware of the fact that one of the greatest characters ever born in Southwestern Virginia first saw the light of day in their village. And this despite the fact that the house in which he was born is still standing in their midst.

One day the writer of this biography visited the Ivanhoe community in search of this early home. It was finally located near the western section of the town. It was occupied by the family of Mr. Garland Jones. But it is no longer the home of a pioneer. With the passing of the years, and with modern ideas of home-building, it has given way to the processes of change.

The original Sheffey home consisted of four rooms of huge logs with a basement underneath. After a visit to the basement, where the logs could be seen, one could not help but be impressed with the fact that those old-time home-builders built for the storms which might beat upon them. They were of massive size and tremendous strength was necessary to place them in position. The basement walls were laid out of heavy stones, and every one of them had evidently been placed in position with the greatest care, for the walls were as strong and as durable as when erected.

But Robert Sayers Sheffey never knew much about this home for his mother passed away a few brief years after his birth. Then it was that he went to Abingdon, Virginia, to live with an aunt. Two brothers—James White and Lawrence—accompanied him. One of these, James White Sheffey, became a great lawyer and a large land owner in Southwest Virginia.

It was while living in Abingdon that Robert S. Sheffey was married the first time. His wife was Miss Elizabeth Swecker, daughter of Wendell Swecker and Rebecca Peters Swecker. The date of the marriage was about the year 1844. To this union six children were born—Daniel Winton, Jonn Robert, James, Hugh Trigg, Margaret Ellen and Sarah Louise. All of these are now dead. There are a number of grandchildren most of whom are living in Wythe county, several of them in the lower Cripple Creek section. Mrs. Sheffey, at her death, was buried in the Painter cemetery on Cripple Creek.

In a conversation with Mrs. Will Neal, of Bluefield, Virginia, it was learned that Sarah Louise Sheffey married an Episcopal minister in Maryland, living near Baltimore. A son of this union also became a rector in the same church in Baltimore. Margaret Ellen at one time lived with her sister near Baltimore. Mrs. Neal is a daughter of James Sheffey and a granddaughter of Robert Sayers Sheffey.

Sheffey had many peculiarities, among these an aversion for education. He had the same privileges of an education that other members of the family enjoyed, but he did not seem to be interested in books and was averse to hard study. One writer says that "he mastered the ordinary branches of an English education, but his early dislike for books and an aversion for profound study followed him all through his long and eventful life." A catalogue published at the end of the first fifty years of Emory and Henry College records the fact that Sheffey was a student at that institution during the years 1839-40. At that time he is listed as an evangelist from Giles county, Virginia. In a letter published elsewhere in these writings he records that Dr. E. E. Wiley, president of Emory & Henry College, Prof. Collins, Mr. Rhea Bogle, and Lawrence B. Sheffey contributed to his education while a student at that institution. He also mentioned a number of other persons who had taught him in his early life.

Chapter III
Robert Sayers Sheffey

Sheffey was about nineteen years of age when he was converted in a revival being held in the town of Abingdon, Virginia, where he had gone to live with some relatives shortly after the death of his mother. From the record it appears that he immediately began work as a missionary among the people of Southwest Virginia. In fact, it was in 1839-40 that he entered Emory & Henry College as a student from Giles county. The conversion of this unusual character dates January 9, 1839. Therefore, it is quite evident that he lost no time in taking up the active duties of an itinerant Methodist preacher. Many of Sheffey's family were members of the Presbyterian church, but he united with the Methodist church because it met with his views in matters of faith and modes of worship.

In a letter written from Lynchburg, Virginia, on July 9, 1897, addressed to Aurelius Vest, at White Gate, Va., Brother Sheffey tells why he happened to unite with the Methodist church. He says that William Sanders, who lived on Kimberling Creek, in Bland county, "got me to join the Methodist church, or was the cause of the same." Sanders "said to me, that Brother Lawrence, (Sheffey's brother), said if I would join the Methodist church he would. I got hold of a discipline and read some of the rules, or all of them, and I went and joined them shortly afterwards." A short time later, in the same letter, Sheffey tells how he visited his relatives at Abingdon, Va., and he goes on to recite something of "the scolding" he got at their hands. "But," he writes "one preacher said to me that I must take a firm stand, a decided stand." Evidently Sheffey did that very thing. He continues, "They said to me this in effect: 'Robert, you ought to have gotten a recommendation to the Methodist church and then joined like a gentleman or an honorable man' ". "This," he said "was the idea with them." He went on: "They wanted me to remain in the Presbyterian church. . . . Perhaps I prayed and cried. . . . I left them and never went back there any more for 14 years, and when I did go back they were dead. I can't say that they died in consideration of me, but they are gone."

After the death of his first wife he became more actively interested in his chosen vocation and his days and nights were given to the work of the Kingdom. He began to reach out into almost every community in Southwest Virginia. It was not long until he was known far and wide as a preacher of the Christian gospel. He had his peculiarities, his idiosyncrasies, his pet hobbies, and his odd whimsical notions, but no man who knew him well ever questioned the sincerity of his life and his faith in God.

His ministry led him into many homes where he met all kinds of people. For these he had the fondest affection and his love for humanity became an obsession with him. He was the friend of white and black alike, and on more than one occasion he shared the hospitality of the colored family who happened to be on his circuit.

On one of his visits to Giles county he stopped over in what is known as "the Irish settlement." This is a community not far removed from the county seat town of Pearisburg. His fondness for this community and its inhabitants later led him to spend the greater portion of his life here among these people. The inhabitants of this community were very largely of Methodist extraction. In fact, one of the first churches built in Giles county had as its cofounder a man who had been ordained by John Wesley in England. His name was Edward Morgan. Descendants of this man are to be found in the neighborhood of Highland church on the New River circuit of the Wytheville district, Holston conference. A recent visit in the home of Robert Morgan, near Belsprings, brought out the fact that Sheffey had often visited in that neighborhood and worshipped at the Highland church.

Mr. Morgan recites that he went, in company with his father, one evening to the Highland church to hear Sheffey preach. Robert Morgan was then a small boy. He said that he left his father and wandered around to the rear of the church and unexpectedly stumbled over Brother Sheffey who was down on his sheep-skin praying. He said he became almost "frightened to death" as he listened to the prayers of the preacher.

Brother Sheffey's visits were always looked forward to with joyous anticipation by the people of the communities where he was accustomed to traveling. He had some peculiarities which were at times annoying to the housewife, but she always knew what to prepare for him for he had the habit of letting everyone know just what he liked most at meal times. The man of the house always knew how to care for his horse for he always told him just how much corn to feed him. And when it was time to retire he let it be known that he always liked a clean bed in which to sleep. But notwithstanding these peculiarities, he was always welcome in any home at which he stopped. And there was a reason. His very presence seemed to leave a benediction of love and peace resting upon every member of the family.

Sheffey's personal habits of cleanliness were well known to everyone with whom he came in contact. Men who knew him mention these things even today.

Lord Bacon in his essay on "Advancement of Learning" says that "Cleanliness of body was ever esteemed to proceed from a due reverence to God." It is very doubtful if Robert Sayers Sheffey ever read a single line of Bacon's writings, but there was an inherent nature that seemed to control all his personal habits of body and mind. He was the avowed enemy of all that was dirty and filthy either in body or mind. No man ever listened to a dirty suggestive story from his lips. He believed that the power of the Christian gospel would cleanse a man of all unrighteousness. His mind was a storehouse of wholesome thought where everything that was impure and unclean was banned altogether. His mind was like that of the Master who never gave utterance to a single thought that was beneath the dignity of the Son of God. He lived on a high plane where purity reigned in supreme authority. "Whatsoever things are true, whatsoever things are honest, whatsoever things are just, whatsoever things are pure, whatsoever things are lovely, whatsoever things are of good report; if there be any virtue, and if there be any praise, think on these things." On this level Robert Sheffey always lived and moved.

John Wesley in his sermon "On Dress," speaking of cleanliness, said: "Certainly this is a duty, not a sin. Cleanliness is indeed next to godliness." Brother Sheffey believed this just as much as John Wesley believed it. No matter where he went, no matter in what circle he moved, he was always scrupulously clean. Those who knew him best remember how strict he was in matters of cleanliness. In many homes where he visited he is remembered by his peculiarities in this direction. He would frown upon anything and everything that smacked of untidiness and uncleanliness. Upon one occasion he wrote, "I think a person should be nice and clean and decent." At many tables where he sat as a guest he would pour out a tablespoonful of coffee into his saucer and after washing the edges of the saucer where the fingers of his hostess had been as she passed the coffee to him walk to the door and throw it out or into the open fireplace. It was a common expression of his that "if you keep the heart right and the skin clean, you won't have any need for lawyers, doctors and penitentiaries."

On one occasion Brother Sheffey was visiting at the home of Mr. and Mrs. Michael Gibson, near Radford, Virginia. At this time a certain woman of the neighborhood dropped into the Gibson home with a small child. The child had been playing out in the yard and its face was quite dirty. Brother Sheffey noticed the child which was crying. He got up from the chair where he was seated, got some soap and handed it to the mother with the admonition: "Now, sister, just take the child and wash the sheep-tangles out of its nose and the dirt off its face, and cool it off, and it will quit crying." At another home where he was a guest, he picked up a tooth-pick and placed it in his mouth and appeared to be picking his teeth. A member of the family happened to be watching him, and when he opened his mouth he discovered that there wasn't a tooth in his head.

He was as careful about his person as a refined woman would be in her make-up for the most auspicious occasion. He never allowed his hands to become soiled in any manner if it was possible to avoid it. He believed that soap and water ought to be applied in no uncertain quantities if one had had occasion to soil their hands or their bodies in any way whatsoever.

A letter which he wrote while stopping at the home of a Mr. Williams, near Pleasant Hill church, in Giles county, reveals many of the idiosyncrasies of this strange man. The letter was written to the editor of The Pearisburgh Virginian, at Pearisburg, in Giles county. It is published in its entirety, forty-odd years and more after it was written, since it is a splendid revelation of the real character of this quaint person:

"Mr. Editor: I am pleased with your present preacher Brother Clemens and his dear affectionate wife and dear sweet children and I wish he and them may find favor with God and man and wish the whole little family well and will get along well and wish that some arrangements can be made to render the house more comfortable than it is, especially during the winter season and I want an arrangement made to get a cow for them, to use as soon as practicable or possible, and an animal for him to ride if the people will; Please Sirs and Madams if neither is yet gotten. They needed both when I was at Pearisburg. I would say to you that I was pleased to preach to the Pearisburg people or citizens when I was there on my last visit, and especially with the following families. The Judge by the name of Porterfield, and his companion and whole family, white or colored man, and Mr. Woolwine, hotel keeper, and Mrs. Wall and family, in consideration of their respect and attention to me every way, I hope he has gotten better than he was when I passed through last, I hope the people will love him and be pleased with him. 'When the righteous are in authority the people rejoice and when the wicked bear Rule the people mourn.' Those last words are God's words. Right here, Mr. Editor, read a few words I say sometimes if every person meaning that can stand it would keep thee or their heart right and their person clean, very clean, there would not be so much need for lawyers, doctors, penitentiaries nor jails. All working persons who labor can't always be clean and nice as other persons may be but at times they may be clean and nice when they go out to church, Sabbath School and into company. There is another thing which has gotten me into a close place in my life in various parts of the world when traveling and that is this, and I know I am right, and right wrongs no man, it has been said. What is it Mr. Wright? Why it is this. I wish every family, bachelor or dear maiden had a good, nice, clean knife to place on the butter plate so that the butter would be clean and pretty on the table, and when it is put away for the next meal. But says one or more, I thought, Sheffey, you are too particular and now I know it. Read a little more here, Mr. Editor. Suppose a man or a person comes to your table who has the typhoid fever, camp scratches, or anything contagious or catching and the person cuts into your butter and gets saliva or spittle on the butter or anything that stains the butter you would perhaps catch whatever disease the person has and would you or any person wish to eat after a filthy person or be near them. My motto is, no sir, I would not; I think a person should be nice and clean and decent, and if the Judge or any person who loves us dearly as I and you love tree molasses or fresh honey, I think they would rather find us nice and clean and decent, especially the lady, if we got into their bed. Another remark or two about kindness and love and affection and hospitality. If anything in the world heads me it is this, when a meeting is closed at night or day for every person too quickly get out of the house or church and after the preacher has preached or exhorted and prayed and sang and no man, woman, or boy, or girl, to step up to the preacher and say to him go home with him or her, such as that is impolite in the extreme. Some persons never say turkey, chicken, opossum nor rabbit to a preacher or a stranger. God says, 'be not forgetful to entertain strangers for thereby some have entertained angels unawares.' It puts me in mind of an Indian and a white man who went hunting together and they killed perhaps a turkey and a crow or buzzard. The white man said to the Indian, you take the crow or buzzard and I'll take the turkey, or else I'll take the turkey and you take the the crow or buzzard, and the Indian said to the white man, you did not say turkey to me either time. Preacher Wiley W. Neal said once the preacher can't live on the wind and every person should cultivate a kind and hospitable and

—43—

affectionate disposition and ways and teach children when young to be so and to be polite and mannered.

"Dear Editor, I want to write a little more for the benefit of the Sugar Run country, &c. I was invited by a Mr. Fortner who used to live perhaps on Sugar Run with a wife and some children. Those who are now alive are full grown. I think I was invited by a preacher on the circuit by the name of Wiley W. Neal to preach on Wednesday perhaps, I went and preached for him, I think, and we perhaps had a meeting that night, and one, two, or three mourners were at the altar of prayer, we had a meeting appointed the next night, and I think I could go near the spot under a tree where my sweet Lord helped me to get something ready to say, and that night I think there was two or three mourners and amongst them was our dearly beloved Sister Susan Stafford, wife of our dear Brother Jno. Edward Stafford a brother of Mess. Monroe and Floy Stafford. I am going to say, Mr. Editor, the people were then on the plain order and a glorious revival bursted out, in that part of the Sugar Run country, and perhaps might have been as great a revival as they ever experienced before that and why so? The Lord converted Mrs. Susan Stafford and the people loved her dearly, and she loved them too, and glory to God, we had some great, grand and glorious times; times of great refreshing to the hearts of the people. I was in that part of the world when the oldest Preacher Farley, Francis Farley and his wife and sons and daughter were yet living, right smart of them are gone to the spirit land or to God who gave them. Look right along where this pen has passed along and you will see something to come next; what is it? There on Brother Farley's premises or plantation I and Eliza W. Sheffey and Eddy F. Sheffey, when a boy, used to live, close to the mill (corn mill) and those Farley people generally saw to me right smartly, especially when I was out laboring for our sweet Lord. Brother Forest Farley and sister Elizabeth his dear wife used to be kind to Eliza and Eddy when I was gone out to work for the people. The old lady Farley was alive when I first went there to live and my family too, John Frank (deceased), helped to see to us and his papa and mother and we had a home there as long as we staid there, and we moved to Staffordsville.

where we now live. And Eddy was mostly educated at Staffordsville. Mrs. Jones, Brother Deck's sister, and Brother Gordon's daughter and Brother Kemp Miller and Mr. or Rev. Wingo, a Christian Baptist preacher, and others may have instructed him and his dear mother helped to raise him. I tried to switch him once and the last time the switch broke and I never tried to switch him any more. I tried to wash him once and he told his mother about it. He said to his mother that I washed him, and washed him, and washed him, and that perhaps was the last washing that I gave to clean him off and his mother and he has seen to him since then. My present wife said to me once Robert, I wish you would quit your foolishness about washing. If these words had been said, Robert, I wish you would just keep on at your splendid plan of washing she would have struck the key note to health and industry and wisdom. Mrs. Elizabeth White who raised me in part taught me to keep clean and go to church, keep out of bad company and read the Bible, commit the Lord's Prayer to memory, corrected me when young and tried to keep me straight, keep the Sabbath day by attending church and Sabbath school. Train up a child in the way he or she should go and when they are old they will not depart from it. My parents, my step mother, three uncles, Col. James White, Jno. White and Alex. White of Abingdon, Washington, Co., Va., and James White Sheffey assisted in raising me, and teachers Mr. Sproles Gillenwaters, and Mr. Pendleton (intemperate), Mr. Sam'l Bailey taught me first and last at Abingdon. Last teacher I ever went to was a Mr. Huggins, and Mr. Hathway or Hathaway, Mr. Shelton and Mr. McVicar at the Academy at Abingdon, Va., Mr. George Washington Buchanan at Marion, Smyth Co., Va., and at college Mr. Rhea Bogle, Brother Lawrence B. Sheffey, Mr. or President Brother Wiley lately (deceased), President Collins also at college. My occupation has been teaching and farming, writing in clerk's office, keeping store, preaching, exhorting, praying all manner of prayer, singing and getting happy and trying to get the sweet Lord to get people on the highest way to glory and to the sweet Lord. If I had always the materials I could cook, milk, churn, wash, iron, make clothing, make up beds, sweep store or house, but could not starch as well as the splendid starchers in the North or East. A young man or lady should be industrious, nice and clean and decent, but not vain, nor proud, but humble. Not too much in love with anything of an earthly nature, but be in love with God and heaven and heavenly things and everything that is right and proper."

Sheffey was the very soul of honor. He never forgot a kindness. If a man dared to offend him, (most men were afraid to do this), he was ready to forgive even seventy times seven.

In a certain community where he was holding a meeting there was a man who refused to invite him into his home because he said, "The old man is too cranky." Brother Sheffey noticed that this man had never given him an invitation to visit in his home. He said nothing about it until the meeting had come to a close. At the final service he prayed, "O Lord, be merciful to that man who never invited me to come into his home." And you may be sure that that man knew whom he was praying for. Other folks did. He might notice any rude treatment, but in his heart there was always a feeling for those who had offended his pride.

Upon one of his preaching tours he came into the little country village of Hillsville, Carroll county, Virginia. His trousers had been torn or ripped in the course of his traveling across the hills and this was noticed by a man in the community who was a sort of tailor. His sympathy was aroused and he suggested to Brother Sheffey that he be allowed to mend the garment. This was done and the good man went on his way. After he had returned to his home he penned a letter to a friend in Hillsville and enclosed a dollar bill asking that it be handed to the tailor for the kindness rendered. When he had finished the letter he added a postscript saying, "Please do not forget to give the dollar bill to the man who fixed my breeches." He was the most appreciative person in the world for a kindness shown to him.

Chapter IV

Robert Sayers Sheffey (Cont'd)

It was on one of his visits to Giles county and the "Irish Settlement" that he met Miss Elizabeth W. Stafford, daughter of J. J. S. and Margaret Stafford, members of a pioneer family of that section. And this young woman later became the wife of Sheffey. She was familiarly known as Eliza to her more intimate friends and associates. It was by this name that her husband always called her, and many are the stories told of her excellent traits of character.

The Stafford family resided in the "Irish Settlement," which is near the community of Staffordsville, on Walker's Creek, about six miles southwest of Pearisburg, the county seat of Giles county. The postoffice was named in honor of this pioneer family. This section boasts of an honorable citizenry and the author was informed by a member of this family, now near the half-century mark, that he had never seen but one or two drunk men in that neighborhood. He also informed me that there had not been a citizen of that community indicted in the courts of Giles county for more than twenty years. The influence of Sheffey's life together with the high type of citizenship in that section speak volumes and are worthy of note in connection with the history of the life of this man of God.

The parents of Eliza Stafford did not look with favor upon the marriage of their daughter to Sheffey because he was in every truth an itinerant preacher of the Word. He never remained very long in any one place. No fault was to be had with his personal life or his family relationships. They could not believe that their daughter would be happy with a man of Sheffey's type as a husband. This was their sole objection to the union, but Sheffey was a determined character and his intentions would brook no interference at any point. He had declared that he would marry Eliza even if he had to marry her on some mountain peak. And so they were married.

Theirs was a perfect union. Edward Sheffey, the only son of this union, declared upon one occasion as he stood at the spot where he was born with uncovered head, "The longer I live the more firmly I am convinced that father made no mistake in his marriage." And he was not alone in this conviction. Even the members of the family who had objected to the union were reconciled to the thought that there was wisdom in that marriage which had united two souls with but a single purpose. Sheffey knew his Bible and he remembered that Jesus had said, "There is no man that hath left house, or brethren, or sisters, or father, or mother, or wife, or children, or lands, for my sake, and the gospel's, but he shall receive an hundredfold now in this time, houses, and brethren, and sisters, and mothers, and children, and lands, with persecutions; and in the world to come eternal life." He was an itinerant Methodist preacher, but he wanted a home, and in this good woman he had - found the pearl of great price who was able to make a home for him and the children who might come of that union. This good woman was in thorough sympathy and full accord with Sheffey in his work. She never murmured or complained at his absence.

There were those who were inclined to criticize Sheffey's absence from his family for such long periods of time. They could not understand how it was that he could absent himself from them for weeks, but it might be said of them that they did not know Sheffey, nor did they know how fully he had sacrificed earthly ties of every description to the God whom he had set out to serve. They could not understand how completely he trusted God in every matter of life, and his family was no exception. The God whom he trusted so implicitly was the God of all mankind. He who noted the fall of the sparrow would not fail him at this point.

Upon one occasion he came home from one of his journeys and his son, Eddy, remarked to him, "Father, uncle Johnny thinks that you ought to spend more time with your family." His reply was, "Son, uncle Johnny doesn't know which way the rats run. The Lord will take care of you." And the Lord did take care of them and they never lacked any good thing. Out of His bounty their needs were supplied.

At first, perhaps, the family of his wife were inclined to criticize his attitude toward his family, but, as the months passed into years, they learned more and more to trust the sincerity of his heart and soul and mind. They discovered how fully committed he was to the work of the Master and they had learned somehow that God had enjoined upon them the responsibility of caring for the earthly needs of his wife and their only son. And they met this responsibility like real men with no complaint upon their part. These men were David C. Stafford, John R. Stafford, and Dr. D. H. Stafford, brothers of Mrs. Sheffey. They saw that every need of the wife and child were met with a smile and a ready heart. After the son had grown to manhood and gone away he would send checks to these uncles to compensate them for their labors in behalf of his mother, but this compensation was unsought upon their part for it had become a source of joy to them to aid the old soldier of the Cross in his labors across his circuit which spread over fourteen counties in Virginia and Southern West Virginia.

The house in which Robert Sheffey and Eliza Stafford Sheffey lived stood in the heart of a beautiful valley not far removed from the present site of Wesley's Chapel, on the Eggleston Circuit of the Methodist church. It is probably seventy-five yards from the home of the late Daily Stafford, a nephew of Eliza, and a man who gave me quite a bit of information given in this writing. It consisted of five rooms. As the writer stood upon the site of that home one day in December, with Daily Stafford, he visualized that time when it was the domicile of the Sheffey family. The outlines of the old house, long since torn away, are clearly apparent. The very spot where the family dug the saltpeter with which to fertilize their vegetables could be seen. The foundations of the old chimneys had not been torn away. To the visitor it seemed that this was a holy place. Here in the simple home a little family had lived and communed with the eternal God. The hush of the hills and the magic of the place combined to make it a real home. It was here that a great mother reared a great and noble son.

Edward Fleming Sheffey, the only child, was born in this home and after reaching manhood's estate he, too, went out into the world to carve a niche for himself and for those who were to follow in his footsteps as a father and as a man of God. Edward Sheffey was a man of God like his sainted father. He inherited all the wealth of character possessed by his father and mother.

Early in life he became a citizen of the thriving city of Lynchburg, Virginia. He identified himself with the Craddock-Terry Shoe Company, one of the major industries of the hill city. He soon became the credit manager of the concern and later vice-president and secretary-treasurer. His efficiency was unquestioned and he soon became one of the outstanding business men of that city. He also identified himself with the Court Street Methodist Church and became an official member of the church board. No man in the whole city was more respected as a citizen, a church man, a family man, and a real Christian. His life was always as sincere and as genuine as that of his sainted father. He was, indeed, "a chip off the old block."

An interesting story is told by a cousin. This particular cousin had invested in properties in the city of Roanoke. His investments promised a handsome return in the way of dividends. His promised success caught the eye of a confidence man who approached him one day with an offer to trade certain stocks for the properties. The owner advised that the properties were not for sale, but the would-be purchaser was persistent and urged upon the owner the wisdom of accepting the tendered stocks in return for a title to the property. Finally the owner asked the man who held the stocks and where he resided, and he said, "In the city of Lynchburg." It was then that the owner asked if he knew Ed. Sheffey. The man in answer to his query said, "Yes, I know him, and there is no better man in Lynchburg. But what do you know about Sheffey?" He was told that Sheffey was a cousin of the owner of the properties. Then it was that the holder of the stocks said, "If you are Sheffey's cousin I would not negotiate further with you in the matter of the sale of your property. I have in my grip stocks which are totaling in prospective value a million dollars, but they are not worth a dime. Because of my respect for Edward Sheffey and his sincerity of character I cannot afford to offer them to you." And with this explanation he walked out of the man's presence. Who will dare say that personal influence does not count in this world of vice and sin? Who will dare say that the spirit of Robert Sayers Sheffey did not brood over that relative of his who might have parted with all his earthly properties of value had it not been for the saintly life he lived?

The Sheffey family, after years of residence in the "Irish Settlement," moved to Staffordsville. Here they lived in a house about one hundred yards above Walker's Creek. The house in which they lived faced the old ford of the creek and many times Sheffey dared the swollen stream and the treacherous ford to get home to his family upon his return from one of his many preaching tours. He never approached the house without taking off his hat for he was the very soul of politeness whether in the home where his family resided or in the home of some of his countless friends across the wide stretches of territory which he traveled.

Sometimes he would ride up to his house and without dismounting call his wife out and talk with her like two children who are infatuated with each other. His greetings were quite brief, and then he would say to his wife, "Eliza, I have got to hurry; I must be at my next appointment." Or, "I have to start a revival" at some point this evening. Sheffey would never loiter at any place. He was always in a hurry. David C. Stafford used to say of him that "He was always in a hurry." When he visited a home he would say almost immediately after his arrival, "Let everybody come into the house for prayer." He lived in the saddle, except for his preaching appointments and his visits into the homes of the people where he visited.

Even in his own home and with his own family his visits were brief. He would stay with his family long enough to sing a song and have prayers and then he would go up to his own room and spend two or three hours in communion with God and he was off again like the courier of the Master.

Edward Sheffey's young manhood was spent very largely around the spot where he first saw the light of day. At Staffordsville he played as a boy and began the development of the fine spirit which dominated all his after life. Here he learned his first lessons and Brother Sheffey recites in a letter how certain persons had contributed to his education. He mentions three persons who taught him as being a Mrs. Jones, a Mr. Miller, and a Baptist preacher by the name of Wingo. He does not forget to mention the part that the mother played in this most important training of the lad.

Young Sheffey moved away from the scenes of his youth-hood while quite immature, but he never lost his interest in the community and the people where he had been born and reared. He rarely ever wrote a letter to any of his relatives but that he included a greeting to "the dear folks of the community." Years later a movement was launched to build a new church at the site of the old structure. Edward Sheffey had a large part in the enterprise and made material contribution to it. A letter to a relative is herewith reproduced to reflect the spirit and the soul of this fine man who had in his life the elements that made his father great in the sight of the Lord and of men in general.

The letter follows without having been deleted in the least respect other than the omission of the name of the party to whom the letter was addressed:

"Herewith please find my check for $100 which is in full of my subscription to the new church at Wesley's Chapel.

"You will remember when I was there and you good people determined to dedicate the church a number of you good folks personally pledged yourselves to raise or pay the balance owing on the church. When the entire amount had been pledged, I stated when you got ready to pay up everything it would be my pleasure to pay $100 in addition to what I had previously pledged, all of which has since been paid except the $100 enclosed which now settles in full. My thought was to pay this $100 and thus reduce proportionately amount each one of you good guarantors had pledged yourselves to see was paid.

"I hope I make myself plain and am pleased to send payment of my final subscription.

"Naturally I love Wesley's Chapel. Being only one mile from my birthplace and where I as a boy knelt at her altars seeking God's favor and pardon and where all that is mortal of my dear father and mother lie buried, it is but natural my mind should frequently revert to those sacred grounds. It is a source of peculiar pleasure to me that you and your associates have, in the Providence of God, been able to build a new church and to improve the surrounding grounds, etc. Keep up the good work.

"Praying God's blessings to be upon you and every one of the workers there, believe me

"Sincerely and affectionately yours,
"Edward F. Sheffey."

This letter is included in this story for the purpose of showing the influence of Robert Sheffey upon his own son and upon the lives of the people in the community where he had spent so many useful years. Edward Sheffey traveled the same path that his sainted father had traveled and served the same God with that same untiring zeal that characterized his father's and mother's lives.

And Brother Sheffey's life did not end with the going down of the sun for the light that shown forth from his own life continued to shine out of the life of Edward Sheffey. And, again, it did not end with the close of Edward Sheffey's day, for out yonder upon the foremost battle lines of the Master's kingdom in darkest Africa, Dr. Charles Sheffey, the son and the grandson, carried on for many years in the name of the Captain of his salvation. "He that liveth and believeth in Me shall never die." Only the eternities will reveal the extent and the fruition of his labors.

While Sheffey's family lived at Staffordsville, he came home one day from one of his journeys to find the creek below his home sweeping on its way in raging torrents as a result of the heavy rainfalls throughout the preceding day and night. A number of inhabitants of the small community were watching the swirling waters and saw Sheffey ride up to the ford unperturbed and undaunted. They called to him and tried to warn him that it would be dangerous to attempt to cross then, but he rode in as calmly as he had ridden down the mountain trail. When he had reached the other side in safety they watched as he dismounted and took his sheepskin and spread it out upon the ground and knelt down to pray. The prayer being over, he mounted his animal and started toward his home. Someone said to him, "Why didn't you pray before you entered the stream?" The answer was typical of Sheffey. It revealed the calm spirit of his soul. "There is no virtue in a scared prayer." He had trusted God many times before, why not trust Him now? God could control the fury of the angry waters. Sheffey knew that and there was not the shadow of doubt in his soul as he rode into the very jaws of death itself on his way to his humble home and his little family who awaited his coming with eager hearts.

 Eliza Stafford Sheffey trusted this man like she trusted God. She believed in him as she believed in the God to whom she had committed her very life together with all that she had in this world. Her faith was as the faith of her husband. Through the centuries there had been countless thousands who had trusted Him. He had not failed them; He would not fail her. While her beloved husband was away on an errand for the Lord she kept vigil over the home and the lad who came into her life to comfort her heart in moments of loneliness. And when the sunset hour had come to her soul she went to sleep like "A dutiful daughter, devoted wife, loving mother and faithful Christian." (Inscription on her monument).

Chapter V

Robert Sayers Sheffey (Cont'd)

On a beautiful October day, in the year 1939, the author visited the city of the dead surrounding the small country church, called Wesley's Chapel, on the Eggleston charge of the Methodist church, Holston Conference. His visit was prompted by a deep desire to look upon the last resting place of this saint of God. A modest and unpretentious grave stone marks the spot where he sleeps until the resurrection morning. The stone reads:

> In Memory of
> Our Father
> Rev. Robert S. Sheffey
> Born
> July 4, 1820
> Died
> August 39, 1902

> Fully consecrated to God's service, he preached the Gospel, without money and without price, and has entered upon his reward.
> The poor were sorry when he died.

But that is not the only monument to his memory. There are innumerable tributes written upon the hearts of his own people as well as the thousands of others who came to a saving knowledge of the Christ through his long years of ministry.

One day the writer dropped in to the North Tazewell Methodist Church, at North Tazewell, Virginia. Upon a stained glass window there had been stamped, "In memory of Brother Sheffey, a man of God whose name in Tazewell County will abide with the years."

In the Huddle-Dunford Sheffey neighborhood in Wythe county, Virginia, there stands a beautiful church, dedicated on June 25, 1905. In this church there is a memorial window which reads: "Our Father, Rev. Robert

S. Sheffey, July 4, 1820. August 30, 1902. Strong in prayer, and in faith, and 'he being dead yet speaketh' ". An account of this dedicatory service is included in these writings.

Through the stifling heat of the summer's day, through the freezing bite of the winter's sleet and ice and snow, this gallant hero of the Cross toiled over this hill-country with the message of redeeming grace and undying love. No wonder men continue to sing his praises for his thoughts were always for others. He was self-sacrificing to the point of destitution. He knew how to be self-denying and how to practice the Christian virtue of unselfishness. He never saw the words of Charles D. Meigs, the author of "Others," but those words are truly applicable to his noble spirit:

> "Lord, help me to live from day to day
> In such a self-forgetful way
> That even when I kneel to pray,
> My prayer shall be for—Others.
>
> "Help me in all the work I do
> To ever be sincere and true
> And know that all I'd do for you,
> Must needs be done for—Others.
>
> "Let 'Self' be crucified and slain,
> And buried deep; and all in vain
> May efforts be to rise again,
> Unless to live for—Others.
>
> "And when my work on earth is done,
> And my new work in Heaven's begun,
> May I forget the crown I've won,
> While thinking still of—Others.
>
> "Others, Lord, yes, others.
> Let this my motto be,
> Help me to live for others,
> That I may live like Thee."

He may never have given utterance to a prayer quite so beautiful in word and thought as this, but his soul was filled with desires that were just as noble, and he was satisfied to "go about doing good" like the humble Galilean who was always his Example. No man knew him but to love him, for he was the brother of every man regardless of race or creed.

Brother Sheffey was always at his best in an old-fashioned Methodist class-meeting where men and women would recount their religious experiences. He boasted of the fact that he had been born twice. He would say, in these meetings, that he was "born of the flesh on July 4, 1820, in Ivanhoe, Wythe county, Virginia, and that he was born of the Spirit on January 9, 1839, over Greenway's store, at Abingdon, Virginia." These were two outstanding events in his life, but he always gave the pre-eminence to the second experience.

Someone has said that "God has a mould for every life, and that when he has drawn the pattern for some He throws the mould away." That must have been true in the case of this life. His was an unusual character. He was peculiar, he was eccentric, but withal a Christian gentleman and no man could find fault with his life. That is, after his second birth. He had caught a vision of a new Ideal and he pursued that Ideal to the end of his life's pilgrimage. He never took his eyes off the Cross which had produced such a reformation in his life and character.

There was one outstanding element in the life of this man. That was his power in prayer. Many persons were afraid of him because he was unaffected by environment or surroundings when he prayed. He talked with God as he would talk with a friend. When he was on his way to church he would tie his horse to an over-hanging limb of a tree and seek seclusion for himself as he held communion with God who was always regarded as omnipotent—having unlimited power—in His every aspect. If there was a desire in his heart he always took that desire to his Father.

In his prayers he always sought to be specific. He called men's names, he withheld nothing, he went to the mercy-seat with an unfaltering faith in the God whom he had met in that old-fashioned revival. He believed with all his heart that what St. John said in his gospel was literally true. He had tried it. To him it was the word of God. "If ye abide in me, and my words abide in you, ye shall ask what you will, and it shall be done unto you." This was not figurative language to him. It was as real as the earth upon which he walked.

A man remarked to the writer some years ago that he would not have had Brother Sheffey to pray against him for the whole world. Another man said that "Brother Sheffey was the most powerful man in prayer that I ever heard, but he couldn't preach a lick."

Men have been at a loss to understand the marvelous power of this man with God in his prayer life. The worldly wise would laugh at his prayers today, perhaps, but Sheffey's wisdom was not of the world. Job said, "Great men are not always wise, neither do the aged understand judgment." Men of the world may marvel at God's ways for "they are past finding out." Paul says that "the preaching of the Cross is to them that perish, foolishness; but unto us which are saved, it is the power of God. For it is written, I will destroy the wisdom of the wise, and will bring to nothing the understanding of the prudent." And, again, Jesus said, "I thank thee, O Father, Lord of heaven and earth, because thou hast hid these things from the wise and prudent, and hast revealed them unto babes." Sheffey laughed at the wisdom of men, but he always marveled at the power of God. It was with the faith of a little child that he approached the "mercy seat" and God never disappointed his faith. He lived within the will of God as his simple faith would allow, and God answered his prayers.

Sheffey was a plain, matter-of-fact sort of preacher. He gave no pretense of having ability to preach. In fact, he was never regarded as having unusual pulpit strength or mannerisms. Many persons have told of his willingness to prostrate himself in the pulpit before the audience as they came into the church, and while lying there engage in prayer with his Father seemingly unconscious of the fact that there was anyone else about.

He hated sham and hypocrisy with his whole heart. He would condemn ecclesiastical dignity in scorching terms and he has brought the blush of shame to the cheeks of many a preacher who prided himself on his rhetoric and his pulpit mannerisms. He attended a meeting in a certain community where there were a number of preachers. These preachers were unable to get up any religious fervor or enthusiasm. They were a rather dignified group of ecclesiastical brethren and Brother Sheffey did not appreciate their attitude toward him. They had paid but scant attention to him and this rather goaded his pride. Now, that they had failed in their efforts to awaken a lethargic congregation, they called upon Brother Sheffey who was "a power in prayer." He started out his petition by telling the Lord that the brethren had failed, and said: "Lord, I think I know what the trouble is. I am sure that the devil is here, and I want you to take him by the nape of the neck, and take him to the edge of the cliff out here, and kick him off." The brethren wilted under the weight of the words of his prayer and the meeting soon became an old-fashioned revival with the power of the Holy Spirit manifest in every direction.

Upon another occasion he was engaged in a revival at the Macedonia church, in Tazewell county. Several young persons were present, and something happened to amuse some of them, and they laughed. This annoyed Brother Sheffey and he said, "Lord, there are some big devils here, and some little devils, and some middle-sized devils. Make them be quiet so that they won't disturb the meeting." That was the end of the laughter. This incident is related by one of those little girls, now married, and with a little girl of her own.

Mrs. C. M. Wagner, of Falls Mills community, near Bluefield, Va., tells of a visit of this peculiar man to the home of her uncle, William Tiller, in Mercer county, W. Va. The Tiller family had a number of bee-hives, and Brother Sheffey was quite fond of honey. He asked Mrs. Tiller if they had any honey and she answered, "No, our bees haven't done any good this spring; they haven't even swarmed." The next morning Brother Sheffey told Mrs. Tiller that they would have plenty of honey in a short time; that the bees would swarm and the gums be filled. In a few days the bees began swarming and in a short time had swarmed seven times. The last swarm settled upon a lettuce stalk.

Jessee Wells, who lived on Bluestone river in Tazewell county, tells the following incident: His father, Robert

Wells, was operating a licensed government distillery high up on the East River mountain, south of where Ebenezer Methodist church, on the Graham circuit, now stands. Sheffey would stop with Wells quite often as he passed through that section. He was very fond of the family, and he always insisted that Wells give up his occupation. A revival was being held at the old Charles' Chapel. One evening Sheffey prayed: "O Lord, I want Robert Wells to quit operating the distillery, but if he won't I want you to cover the face of the mountain with ice and cause Wells to slip and fall coasting down the mountain side into hell before he goes much farther. His business is ruining the men of this community. Make him quit." The result was that Wells quit his job, the distilling plant was torn out, and that was the end of Wells' connection with the liquor traffic.

Another time Sheffey was at the Wells home, and Robert Wells was engaged in logging huge trees off the mountain side. During the operation of the industry, Wells had the misfortune to get his foot caught between the wagon wheel and a stump. The foot apparently was badly injured, but Brother Sheffey said he would pray about it, and in a few days Wells was out walking around. What had appeared to be a permanent injury proved to be nothing more than a slight injury and did not incapacitate Wells for work more than a few days.

Sheffey's ministry was not unlike that of John the Baptist, the fore-runner of Jesus, in that he drew men from the high places and the low places. The high and the low were his friends and his power was irresistible in the pulpit and in the homes where he found shelter. He was the guest of the rich planter as well as the humble tenant. When Brother Sheffey was coming every door was open to him. He was welcomed as a prince of Israel and he never left a home without leaving the smile of heaven upon that home. And when it was noised abroad in a community that Brother Sheffey was a guest in a certain home, it was not long before that home was deluged with visitors who came to see and to hear this man who went about only to do good.

One is reminded of the many experiences of the Master who was thronged and pressed by the multitudes of people who eagerly hung their hopes upon the beneficient words that fell from his lips. An elderly lady tells the story of a visit that Brother Sheffey made to the home of her parents in her girlhood days. While the family was having its evening meal friends throughout the countryside who had heard of the presence of the man of God came with their children and sat out in the yard underneath an apple tree to talk with the old saint. As he got up from the table he took two table-spoonfuls of sugar in his hands and filled his mouth with it as he went into the yard. He sat down among the people and his first audible words were "sweet Jesus." Then he began to talk with them about the deep things of life, and before the throng had dispersed they were seen to be weeping on every side. "Heaven came down to crown the mercy seat" and the people sat together in "heavenly places in Christ Jesus." He did not seem to know how to talk to people about things that pertained to the temporal side of life. His thoughts were high and holy and never on the level of the suggestive or common-place things of life. His citizenship was in heaven, and he talked like a resident of that place. He did not have time to spend on the trivial and the trifling affairs of life. These were for men and women of the world and not for one who had the weight of the sins of a lost world weighing upon his soul.

He was not unlike Enoch of old in that he walked and talked with God. Inspiration for his God-like life came from those walks and talks with that One who had said that He would be with him "always, even unto the end of the world."

Interesting, but true, is the statement that this veteran of the Cross never took his eyes off that Cross. To him that Cross with all of its blood-bathed gospel was ever "the power of God unto salvation to every one that believeth." With upreaching heart he went on his way with that gospel ploughing the soil, sowing the seed, and reaping the harvest. He did not plough in vain, he did not sow in vain, but the harvest has not yet been reached in its entirety. There are scores of men and women who point with a feeling of pride to his ministry and to the gospel he preached with indefatigable earnestness and untiring energy. Somehow, in his call to preach, he had learned a lesson that many men of the itineracy have never understood. He knew how to labor and not be wearied out; he had learned how not to yield to fatigue; he had seen the Master and in those eyes he understood how to be unremitting in labor and effort.

Out of the silences he drew strength of body and soul. He lifted his eyes unto the hills of God where there were unlimited sources of power for the hearts of the children of men who knew the way of the Cross. As he rode across the hills, down through the valleys, over the wild mountain passes, along the sides of the swollen streams searching for a place where he might cross in safety to the other side to be on his way as "the Courier of the Long Trail," he breathed a prayer in his humble heart and trusted God to make the way clear and the dangers less imminent. His was the courage of the prophet and the soul of the priest of God. He verily believed that where God called him to go there were no dangers but that He would assume for Himself and they were not for him who dared to go. God's promises were his promises. They would brook no denial. No matter how great the need, no matter how dangerous the road that lay ahead, no matter how many obstacles the world might lay across his path, only God counted. Nothing else mattered. R. Keene, wrote a hymn that became the anchor of his soul. It made the way easier. It follows:

"How firm a foundation, ye saints of the Lord,
Is laid for your faith in His excellent word.
What more can He say than to you He hath said,
You who unto Jesus for refuge have fled?

"In every condition—in sickness, in health;
In poverty's vale, or abounding in wealth;
At home and abroad; on the land, on the sea—
As thy days may demand, shall thy strength ever be.

"Fear not: I am with thee; O be not dismayed,
I, I am thy God, and will still give thee aid;
I'll strengthen thee, help thee, and cause thee to stand,
Upheld by my righteous, omnipotent hand.

"When through the deep waters I call thee to go,
The rivers of woe shall not thee overflow;

For I will be with thee, thy troubles to bless,
And sanctify to thee thy deepest distress.

"When through fiery trials thy pathway shall lie,
My grace, all-sufficient, shall be thy supply;
The flame shall not hurt thee;—I only design
Thy dross to consume, and thy gold to refine.

"E'en down to old age, all my people shall prove
My sovereign, eternal, unchangeable love;
And when hoary hairs shall their temples adorn,
Like lambs they shall still in my bosom be borne.

"The soul that on Jesus still leans for repose,
I will not, I will not, desert to his foes;
That soul, though all hell should endeavor to shake,
I'll never, no never, no never forsake."

 Men do not know how to fail—men who know how to sing that song in their hours of deep soul need. It is the song of the victor. Those who fail have never learned its strength and beauty. There are always the everlasting arms underneath.
 Large circuits are always the bane of the modern-day preacher. There are too many miles to travel; there are too many points on the charge; there are too many arduous tasks to perform. But Brother Sheffey's circuit reached across most of the counties of Southwestern Virginia and Southern West Virginia. He preached in Bland, Wythe, Giles, Grayson, Tazewell, Smyth, Washington, Montgomery, Floyd and Carroll counties in Southwest Virginia, and Mercer, McDowell, Monroe, and Summers counties in Southern West Virginia. Fourteen counties in all! Wherever men and women came together to learn the art of prayer and soul-communion with their God Sheffey found time to pause and pray with them.
 It was in the autumn. The mountain-sides were covered with their golden tints. The shadows of the evening-time were lengthening across the hills when this gentle soul came into the little mountain village of Independence, Grayson county, Virginia, and stopped to spend the night in a neighbor's home. The writer was then a small lad. He had heard of "Brother Sheffey," and in his childish play he

dropped into this home to see this strange looking little man with beard-covered face. In the old-fashioned parlor he found him and as he peered around the door facing he saw an unusual sight—a man down on a sheep-skin praying. With upturned face he looked toward the heavens and his face was aglow with an unearthly light. That picture has never faded from his memory, and on an October afternoon, with the mountain-sides once again painted in their most artistic colors, that same lad, now a man, stood by the tomb of this old man, sleeping his last sleep, and with uncovered head prayed that that same spirit of prayer might dominate and possess his own life.

I remember seeing that old sheep skin upon which he knelt in that home. It was brought to a church service where I was preaching and was the prized possession of Joseph Davidson of Nemours, W. Va., over in Mercer county. It may have been a worthless possession as one considers its monetary value, but no money could buy it. It had faded with the years; it had grown yellow; it had many corners cut from it for keepsakes; it was just an old faded, yellowish looking sheep-skin, but there was something about it that makes one tremble as he fondles it. It talks, it whispers, it prays, it sings, it shouts, it laughs, it cries. It is an eerie something—lonely, weird, gloomy, mysterious. Out of the past it speaks to those who would hear. It whispers with that same voice that knew how to pray, and sing, and shout, and laugh, and cry.

Brother Sheffey, as he visited in the homes of the people across the wide stretches of his self-appointed circuit, never allowed an opportunity to pass without praying with the family and with those who may have been guests in that home. He would also read the Scriptures for he saw in them the words of eternal life. His favorite book was that of the Psalms. He seemed to have found in the words of the writers of that book the encouragement for his own soul, and he believed that that same encouragement would suffice for others. Many times he would open the Book and read a few verses and then pass on to other verses. He rarely ever read a chapter entirely through. And he would almost invariably turn to the book of Psalms before he had completed his reading.

He was also very fond of singing. The old gospel hymns were always an unfailing source of joy to his soul. He had a striking peculiarity in his manner of singing. He would square his shoulders and place his right hand against his cheek and then "he lifted the tune" until the whole audience were joining in the singing with him. The song he sang more often than any other was "Blessed Be the Name of the Lord." And if anyone else was leading the singing in one of his services they remembered that this was his favorite hymn and before the service had come to a close this hymn was sung. He would often write snatches of the hymn upon objects along the mountain trails which he traveled and on the walls of the homes where he happened to be stopping.

The travels of this eccentric itinerant were almost unbelievable. If any way of reckoning the miles he traveled across the years was at all possible one would be amazed. He would sometimes travel with the preachers in the territory he traversed, but more often he would go alone. He sought only the counsel of God and this he found in the solitudes as he journeyed over this hill country. Wherever he met a man he would seek a word with him and before he had gone on his way he would pray for that one lone soul.

He looked upon men with a feeling of compassion in his heart for them and their sinful condition. He was the brother of every man regardless of race and creed. He believed that Jesus died for all mankind and that the Spirit of the Master made him the kinsman of every man in the wide, wide world. He was like an eminent divine who was asked if he would baptize a "nigger." His answer was, "I'll baptize any man whom Jesus died for." He would preach to any man, pray for any man, agonize with any man who was an heir of this salvation. No man was too humble, no man too mighty, to excite his interest and concern. A soul was a priceless possession in the sight of God and so it was to him.

Many are the stories that are told regarding his interest in his fellow-man. One story has it that he had been given a heavy pair of woolen socks by a lady on "his charge." It was a cold winter day and as he went on his way he met a mailcarrier. The man appeared to be thinly clad and this appealed to his fatherly nature. He thought the man was likely to get cold on his journey and so he urged him to accept the gift of the socks which had so recently been given to him. The mailman accepted the gift rather reluctantly and after placing them on his feet took up his journey. Brother Sheffey went on his way and stopped with a nearby family and told them of his act of beneficence when they discovered that his feet were bare. His generosity did not go unrewarded for he soon had another pair of woolen socks to take the place of the ones he had given away.

He had an undying hatred for the liquor traffic. He always spoke out against it in his sermons and in his prayers. He would call the names of men who were engaged in the liquor business in his prayers and urge God to cause them to give up their traffic in the business or take them out of the community. He "prayed out" many a devastating business of this nature and closed the places where liquor was being manufactured.

One day he and Rev. John M. Romans, for many years a respected member of the Holston conference of the Methodist church, were traveling over one of the mountain ranges in a county of Southwestern Virginia. One of them sighted a spiral of smoke winging its way out of a deep mountain hollow. They soon decided that this must be the rendezvous of a mountain moonshiner. Their horses were stopped and Brother Sheffey got down and prayed that God might send a mighty torrent of rain that would wash out that hollow and destroy the plant of the illicit distillery. They remounted their horses and rode on for a short distance when Brother Sheffey remarked that it would not be long before God would intervene. In about an hour's time a heavy rainfall came and swept the hollow from one end to the other washing out the entire plant and frightening the operators almost to death. Brother Romans told the story many times and remarked that when Brother Sheffey began to pray there was not the slightest evidence of a cloud in the sky anywhere.

On another occasion he was holding a meeting in a certain county in this same area and there was a distillery not so many miles distant from the church. Brother Sheffey prayed that a tree might fall across the plant and destroy it and that the foundation stones about it be turned into a pig-sty. A short time later that very thing happened. A tree fell across the distillery and it required many men to remove the fallen monarch of the forest. The plant was crushed into the earth and the very foundation stones were used to make the sides of a pig-sty.

He had no patience with sin in any form and was the avowed enemy of all works of the devil, but in his sympathies and his compassion he was as tender and as gentle as a woman. He could not stand idly by and see even the least of God's creatures injured or destroyed. He was a lover of every form of nature and many interesting and sometimes laughable stories are told of the thoughtfulness of this saint toward "even the least" of God's creation.

One day he was visiting at the home of a friend up Wolfe Creek, from Narrows, Va. The water in the creek was quite low owing to a drouth which had been long felt in that territory. On his way up to the home he had to cross the stream and he discovered that the water had receded in one place and left hundreds of tadpoles in a little pool where they would soon die. Brother Sheffey got down off his horse and took his handkerchief out of his pocket and made a small seine which he used to transfer these tiny creatures back into the main body of the stream. He did this many times in his journeys up and down this hill country.

On another occasion he was stopping in the home of Mr. and Mrs. Martin Lundy at Independence, Grayson county, Va. In the evening as the family and their guest were seated before the open fireplace the hostess got up and placed a doty piece of wood on the fast dwindling fire. Hundreds of large ants began to crawl out of the wood and Brother Sheffey took his knife and bored a hole in the hearthstone and soon every one of the tiny creatures had crawled down through that hole into safety.

A relative by marriage tells an interesting story about a weasel which had been captured in the barn at the Sheffey home. The weasel had been killing some of the chickens and a trap had been placed in the barn where the chickens roosted. That night the marauder was captured and when Brother Sheffey went out to the barn he discovered that it was being held by its front feet and that both of them had been broken by the jaws of the trap. He carried the little animal out to the woodshed and took the axe and chopped off its head. This same relative says that this is the only time that he ever knew him to harm any kind of an animal. The reason he gave was that it was hopelessly wounded and that it would suffer less to have its head chopped off than to travel the rest of its days with broken legs.

Another time while riding along the road in Grayson county, Virginia, on Elk Creek, he discovered a tumble-bug on its back. He got down from his horse, turned the bug over, and went on his way.

Daily Stafford says that Sheffey was "the very soul of affection and love for everything and everybody." He remembers to have seen him more than once as he moved along with a funeral procession to drop out of that procession and get off his horse to lift a bug out of a wagon trail where it might be killed. He says that he had seen him frighten a snake up the hill or toward its hole so that it would not be killed by someone who had less regard for his snakeship. He didn't like to see even a snake killed or injured.

And speaking of snakes we are reminded of another story which has to do with a rattlesnake. Sheffey was traveling up Wolfe Creek, in Giles county, when word came to him that he was wanted at a certain home because a member of that family had been bitten by a rattlesnake and there was reason to suspect that the bite might prove fatal. The family had such confidence in Sheffey's prayers that they believed that he might be able to save the lad who had been bitten. Arriving at the home, he asked if he had been sent for and when advised that he had a member of the family requested that he might pray for "George," the boy who had suffered the bite. He slowly got down upon his knees and began his prayer in this vein: "O Lord, we do thank Thee for rattlesnakes. If it had not been for a rattlesnake they would never have called upon You. Send a rattlesnake to bite Bill, and one to bite John, and send a great big one to bite the old man." A man over at Narrows gave me this story.

Brother Sheffey knew how to suit his prayers to almost

any sort of a situation. He could use words to bite like a scorpion when he prayed, and, then, again, he could be as sweet and as simple as a little child. He was "instant in season and out of season" in the matter of prayer.

Upon another occasion he was visiting in the home of a man who was not a Christian. He urged the man to give his heart to the Lord and unite with the church, but his insistence had fallen upon deaf ears. After having spent the night with the family of this man, the next morning he started to the barn to get his horse. His host accompanied him to the barn as is the custom among the hill people. Once more he urged his host to give his heart to Jesus and unite with the church. The man said, "Alright, Brother Sheffey, the next time I have an opportunity I will do what you have requested me to do." Brother Sheffey replied, "That's fine; we'll do it right here. I will get my discipline and open the door of the church if you will settle the matter. Now is the time." And with this he began to sing and pray with the man who was finally converted, and he then received him into the church.

Another time he was riding along the road and met a man. He stopped his horse and told the man that he was about to begin a revival at the nearby church and gave him an invitation to attend the services. The man said he would do so if he could get a pair of trousers that were decent to wear to church. Brother Sheffey opened his saddle-bags and pulled out an extra pair of trousers that he was carrying with him and gave them to the man saying, "I'll be looking for you tonight."

One evening he stopped at the Frank Priddy home in Narrows and after reading the word of God he called the family to prayer. A neighboring child was visiting in the home. In his prayer he said of this little girl, "God bless the little girl with the red joisey (blouse) on, and God bless Tommy. We want them to get married." And they did. That little girl became the bride of the Rev. Thomas Priddy, for many years a useful member of the Holston conference, and in his latter years an outstanding evangelist of the Methodist fraternity.

There are literally thousands of stories told about his manner of prayer and the answers that came in response to those prayers. If these stories could all be gathered together men would open their eyes in wonderment.

The story which follows came from the lips of a man who had heard his father recite it over and over again. Near the Sheffey home, in "the Irish settlement," there lived a neighbor who was visited quite often by this quaint character. Sheffey had ridden up to the home and placed his horse in the barn remaining at the home for some time thereafter. A new gate had recently been erected at the barn. To get his horse it was necessary to go through this gate. When the time came for his departure he sent a member of the family out to the barn for his horse. A new locust post had been planted at the gate and a hole bored into the post for a pin which held the gate in place. During his visit a heavy rain had fallen and the pin was swollen until it was next to impossible to remove it. The young man who had gone for the horse came back to the house and said he could not remove the pin so as to open the gate. The old man quietly walked out to the gate with his umbrella over him, for it was still raining, and after lifting his hat and bowing his head for a moment in silent prayer, he took hold of the pin, pulled it out, and got on his horse and rode away without saying even a word.

It is interesting to note how men have remembered his prayers through the years. When other incidents have been forgotten the things for which he prayed a quarter or a half century ago come leaping out of the darkness like a phantom ghost. A visit in the home of a friend brought forth an interesting story of a prayer which was answered long years afterward.

Over in Wythe county, Virginia, near the site of the old Asbury camp meeting ground, lived a man by the name of Scott. He owned a place where he sold liquor and the business had become a source of evil in that section. Brother Sheffey often visited in that community and he saw the results of the liquor traffic upon the people of the neighborhood. This excited his concern for he was always the avowed enemy of every business of this nature. In a religious service he talked to the Lord about the matter, He asked that the home of Scott might become the home of a Methodist preacher and that the still-house where the liquor was made might be remodeled and made into a barn for the preacher's horse and that the trough would be turned into a trough where the preacher's horse would be fed.

The years passed by and the prayer was almost forgotten. When the Rural Retreat circuit was about to be divided and the Cedar Springs circuit formed the Scott place was bought by the church people and the homes remodeled into a home for the pastor of the Cedar Springs circuit. Some carpenters were called in and they, in company with some members of the circuit, were converting the still-house into a barn. They were also using the trough in which the still-worm had lain to make a trough for the preacher's horse. Suddenly and unexpectedly someone of those present remarked, "Well, this is the answer to the prayers of Brother Sheffey." And then he recited the story of his prayer in the religious service in the neighborhood many years prior to that time.

This story is told by Rev. L. W. Pierce, district superintendent of the Methodist churches in the Tazewell district at the time he related it to me. His father who was a member of the Sugar Grove, (Virginia), congregation had sent him up to the Scott place to aid the men in their work. At that time he was a lad about seventeen years of age. The incident made a profound impression upon his mind and he had remembered the circumstances under which the answer came to Sheffey's prayer.

There are those who will say that these things just never happened. But they did happen. And the explanation is to be found in the fact that Sheffey never did anything without first talking to God about it. Even the seemingly unimportant things of life were important enough to him to be brought to the attention of his Father. He made his business the Father's business, and the Father's business was the only concern of his life.

One day he was traveling along the road and stopped at the home of Peter Hardiman, near Staffordsville, Va. Mrs. Hardiman had a flock of geese. It was a hot sultry day and the geese appeared to Brother Sheffey to be unhappy. They were penned up near the house and he asked Mrs. Hardiman why she kept them in pens with water so near at hand. She told Brother Sheffey that the geese wanted to set and that she had tried in every way to stop them from doing so, even going to the extreme point of putting sharp rocks in their nests so as to make their nests uncomfortable. Sheffey said he would pray about it. He did. And the result: The geese never attempted to set again.

Another time he stopped at the Hardiman home. Mr. Hardiman was engaged in digging a well. He had been digging for days but there was no water in sight and he had just about decided to abandon the work and start digging at another place. Brother Sheffey said, "Let me talk to the Lord and see what He says about it." He prayed and then he said, "The Lord says to keep on digging. You will have plenty of water after awhile." Hardiman kept on digging and finally he struck water and the well actually flowed over. He had struck a stream of water that was ever-flowing.

Brother Sheffey was visiting in the home of George Stafford one day in the fall when the wasps were crawling about the windows and dropping on to the floors threatening to sting the members of the family. Mr. Stafford picked up the scissors and walked over to the window and cut one of them into pieces. Sheffey did not say anything but in a little while he went out into the yard. Mr. Stafford followed him and discovered him down in the corner of the chimney praying. He said, "Robert, what are you doing?" His answer was, "I am praying for the Lord to make another wasp to take the place of the one you killed."

Another time he was passing through a certain section where there was a very severe drouth. The crops appeared to be dying and cattle were suffering from lack of water. It was a very serious situation to the people of that part of the countryside. Sheffey stopped his horse and went up into the woods to pray. He urged the Lord to send rain and save the crops and the stock of the people from the perils of the drouth. There was no sign of rain anywhere at the time, but a few hours later clouds began to form and soon the rain descended upon the land and relief came to the impoverished crops and stock. One day after another it was like this to Sheffey. But these things were commonplace experiences to him. God was his daily companion and he talked with Him as he traveled across the hills engaged in the Master's business.

Daily Stafford says that Sheffey received almost countless numbers of letters and requests from people to pray for certain things in which they were interested. Sometimes it was a lost boy, sometimes it was someone who was ill, sometimes it was for some person in need of material help, sometimes it was for someone who was desperately in trouble. Sheffey always remembered these requests when he prayed.

There was a certain family in a nearby community who were not very consistent in their manner of Christian living. Their names were Cottrell. (They are now dead). A revival was being held in that neighborhood and, as usual, the Cottrells came to the altar and were converted over again. This was a common occurrence and Sheffey knew it. After this new "heart-warming experience" Sheffey prayed, "Lord, bless the Cottrells; kill 'em and take 'em home while the fur is good." Sheffey knew that there were certain seasons of the year when the furs of animals were good; at other times it was worthless so far as the markets went. This was what he referred to when he said, "take 'em home while the fur is good."

He was holding a meeting in the neighborhood of Narrows, Virginia, in Giles county, upon one occasion and one evening while on his way to church he met a man by the name of Harve Frazier. He suggested to Frazier that he come to the services the next day. The man replied that he would like to attend the meeting, but that every time he left home the hogs would get into his cornfield and destroy his corn. Brother Sheffey said to him, "You come on to church tomorrow, the hogs won't bother your corn any more." Frazier went to the meeting and the hogs never bothered his cornfield again.

One day Captain Wm. Henry Staples, a lawyer residing at Narrows, Giles county, was on his way over to Bland courthouse where he also practiced his profession. Traveling up the mountain in the direction of Bland he noticed some person in the distance, ahead of him, who appeared to be walking back and forth across the road. Riding up he recognized Brother Sheffey. He said, "Mr. Sheffey, what

—73—

are you doing?" Sheffey replied, "Mr. Staples, I found some tadpoles here by the side of the road in a mud-hole which was almost dried up. I have been carrying water across the road to put in the mud-hole so the tadpoles will not die." When the task was completed he got on his horse and rode with Staples. When the lawyer arrived at Bland he immediately went into the courthouse where court was already in session. Brother Sheffey walked in an hour or two later and proceeded directly up to the bar saying, "Captain Staples, don't forget the tadpoles," turned on his heel and walked out seemingly unconscious of the fact that he was in a court of justice where people were expected to be quiet and orderly and undue talking was likely to be followed by a stern rebuke upon the part of the presiding officer.

Whenever Sheffey entered into a home he always took his time about praying and observing the mannerisms of a polite guest. He did not like for even members of the family to appear to be indifferent or callous toward his Master's work. In fact, he would not hesitate for one moment to rebuke anyone who interfered with his plans in this direction. It is said that upon one occasion he and the late Rev. J. Tyler Frazier and another minister whose name has been forgotten were on their way to some church meeting. Two day's travel were required in getting to the scene of the meeting. They, of course, were required to stop on their way for meals and a place at which to spend the night. Brother Sheffey took up so much time in his devotions with the families where they stopped that the other brethren became somewhat irked and embarrassed. They held a conference between themselves in which they decided that they would rush things along the morning after they had spent a night in a certain home. They knew Sheffey's habits and knew that he would likely go into the woods to pray before coming back to the home to have devotions with the family before they were to depart. The two preachers rushed to the barn and curried the horses and led them to the front of the house and then went into the house taking their seats while they waited the return of their companion from the nearby woodland. In a short time they heard quite a commotion outside the house and rushed out to discover that their two horses had broken their reins and rushed off down the road while Sheffey's horse stood at the post where he had been hitched as quiet and as calm as if nothing had happened. About this time Brother Sheffey walked up and met the two brethren saying to them, "I went up yonder to pray and I saw the sweetest little rabbit as it ran across the pathway. I wish you could have seen it. It would have made your hearts happy." He never said a word about the horses. The men finally captured their horses and then they went back into the house and Brother Sheffey quietly remarked, "We will now have prayers." Brother Frazier, telling of the incident, said, "We decided then and there to never interfere again with Sheffey's plans for prayer."

Things like these were common occurrences in his everyday life. He treated them as common-place happenings and even though they may have appeared grotesque to others there was nothing unusual or extraordinary about them as far as he was concerned.

He was holding a meeting in the Hale's Chapel neighborhood, near Narrows. Someone invited him to go home with them for dinner. They set down at the table and Brother Sheffey observed a big fat hen on the table. Of course, Sheffey was asked to say the blessing. He said, "O Lord, we thank Thee for the beautiful chicken on the table, but it would have been much better if they had made dumplings with it." And who wouldn't have felt like Sheffey?

Newberry's Chapel, in Bland county, was the scene of many of the religious activities of Brother Sheffey. He liked to visit in this neighborhood because he was received into the homes of the various families of the community with friendly greeting and unalloyed respect. Allen T. Newberry was one of his most loyal friends. Newberry happened to be the son of Samuel Newberry, one of the pioneer preachers of the Methodist church in Southwestern Virginia. This preacher once served a charge that reached from Saltville, Virginia, in Washington county, to Eaton's Chapel, in Giles county. He believed in the Methodist church and his brand of courage made possible the foundations of Methodism in this hill country. His son, Allen, had the same spirit of loyalty toward the church of his father's faith. He became a great admirer of Brother Sheffey for they had many things in common. Newberry was a wealthy citizen and he would make a trip to Baltimore about once a year with a load of cattle for the markets. He would usually bring back with him a whole bolt of English broadcloth out of which his suits were tailored. He would always see to it that Brother Sheffey had a suit of the same material. That attachment between them was quite marked.

Upon one occasion, when Sheffey was visiting in the neighborhood of Bland courthouse, he stopped at the home of William M. Williams. About this time Martin Williams, who later became one of the outstanding lawyers of Southwestern Virginia, was desperately ill of typhoid fever. Several physicians had been called in for consultation. The young man was given up to die. When Brother Sheffey heard of his condition he immediately began to pray for the recovery of the youth. Finally, he went to Mrs. Williams and advised her that there was no need for further alarm, that the patient would recover. In a very brief time he began to improve and in a short time was entirely well again. This story was given to the writer by Mrs. Martin Williams, widow of the distinguished Virginians, and a granddaughter of Allen Newberry, who was residing at Pearisburg at the time she told me the story.

Chapter VI

Brother Sheffey's Great Faith

The worth of a man's life may be reckoned from the opinions of others who know him and are able to separate the straw from the chaff. Sheffey made a profound impression upon those who were touched by his life and character. Herewith we reproduce articles from books, newspapers, and individuals. These speak for themselves.

His regular preaching place in Mercer county was close to the home of Anderson Tiller. One incident, verified by Mrs. James White, a daughter of Mr. Tiller, is a real "Believe It or Not" oddity. On one occasion, when Preacher Sheffey was dining in the home of the Tillers, the head of the house explained that he had no honey to offer him. Apparently the cold weather had destroyed the bees. Sheffey, a lover of sweets, fell on his knees and beseeched the Lord to help him in the dilemma. His prayer was answered in a very brief time. Swarms of bees came, and there was plenty of honey for all.

"I'll just go and talk to the Lord," said Sheffey when he needed guidance. His prayers were almost always answered.—The Semi-Centennial Edition of the Bluefield Daily Telegraph of 1889-1939.

The Thorn Spring Methodist Church, in Pulaski county, was a favorite place with Brother Sheffey. Quoting from the centennial edition of The Southwest Times of 1939, (article written by Mrs. Wooling), we read:

"This old church can be seen just back of the barn on Col. Harman's estate. This old building is a ruin now, and is like an old skeleton with its sightless eyes. On the land adjoining the church on the late Thomas Ingles' land are the old oak trees with horse shoes in them, where the horses used to be hitched. This should be sacred ground to many whether Methodist or other denomination, for it was there many of their fore-fathers worshipped. It was the custom of the nearby inhabitants in those days to gather there during the camp meeting season, camp, and extend hospitality to those who came from a distance.

"One of the unique characters who used to frequent these meetings was the Rev. Robert Sheffey. He was a missionary to the people of the mountains, a Methodist after John Wesley's own heart. In a series of articles, he was written up by a member of another denomination. I quote a short paragraph—'He traveled thousands of miles through all kinds of weather, ate and slept in hundreds of homes. He prayed and read to them the Scriptures. The people loved him and believed in his sincerity. His life was an open book, and they recognized him as being an epistle of Christ. He believed in the Bible from 'kiver to kiver,' was not bothered with higher criticism.'

"Long live the memory of Robert Sheffey, the mountain evangelist and typical Methodist circuit rider. We smile in a superior way at the stories told of him, many of which are true, but his influence for good lives on. His immediate family show the influence of his Godly life, his son 'Eddie' as I have heard him call his son, died not long since. He was one of the most influential members of the Court Street Methodist church in Lynchburg as well as a respected and honored citizen of that city.

"Brother Sheffey has a grandson, Dr. Charles P. M. Sheffey, son of 'Eddie,' who is a medical missionary in Africa, and was supported by his father in the work as long as he lived.

"Dr. Sheffey returned to America on a furlough in 1938, and a number of Pulaskians were fortunate to attend a service at Wytheville where he spoke.

"Col. King Harman had a phonographic record on which a prayer and a song of Brother Sheffey is recorded."

A letter was addressed to Mrs. King Harman asking for a copy of the song and prayer. She replied: "My husband did have the record and prayer of Rev. Sheffey, but one cold winter day he was playing it for someone, and it cracked to pieces, so it is no good. We were so sorry to have lost it, for it was perfect."

George C. Rankin, D. D., for several years a member of the Holston and Texas Conference, met Sheffey while a pastor of the Wytheville station and circuit in the middle seventies. Rankin was a great preacher as preachers were measured in those days. He served the Wytheville,

Abingdon, Knoxville (Church Street), and Market Street churches of Methodism. In the early nineties he wrote "The Story of My Life" in which he records his impressions of Sheffey whom he first met at the famous Cripple Creek campground which was on the Wytheville circuit. He has this to say of Sheffey:

"The rarest character I ever met in my life I met at that camp meeting in the person of Rev. Robert Sheffey, known as 'Bob' Sheffey. He was recognized all over Southwest Virginia as the most eccentric preacher of that country. He was a local preacher; crude, illiterate, queer and the oddest specimen known among preachers. But he was saintly in his life, devout in his experience and a man of unbounded faith. He wandered hither and thither over that section attending meetings, holding revivals, and living among the people. He was great in prayer, and Cripple Creek camp ground was not complete without 'Bob' Sheffey. They wanted him there to pray and work in the altar.

"He was wonderful with penitents. And he was great in following up the sermon with his exhortations and appeals. He would sometimes spend nearly the whole night in the straw with mourners; and now and then if the meeting lagged he would go out on the mountain and spend the entire night in prayer, and the next morning he would come rushing into the service with his face all aglow shouting at the top of his voice. And then the meeting always broke loose with a floodtide.

"He could say the oddest things, hold the most unique interviews with God, break forth in the most unexpected spasms of praise, use the homeliest illustrations, do the funniest things and go through with the most grotesque performances of any man born of woman.

"It was just 'Bob' Sheffey, and nobody thought anything of what he did and said, except to let him have his own way and do exactly as he pleased. In anybody else it would not have been tolerated for a moment. In fact, he acted more like a crazy man than otherwise, but he was wonderful in a meeting. He would stir the people, crowd the mourners' bench with crying penitents and have genuine conversions by the score. I doubt if any man in all that conference (Holston) has as many souls to his credit in the Lamb's Book of Life as old 'Bob' Sheffey."

Dr. Rankin in the above statement regarding Sheffey's peculiarities refers to him as being "crude," "illiterate," etc. It is true that Sheffey was peculiar and eccentric, but few men have had the audacity (daring) to say of him that he was "illiterate," or "crude." Nor was he educated in the sense in which we moderns of today think of education. But, after all, in the words of Dr. John G. Hibben, former president of Princeton University, "Education is the ability to meet life's situations." How well Sheffey was prepared to do this is revealed by the achievements of his life.

The converts of Sheffey can be counted by the hundreds and perhaps thousands. Among these are men who have been outstanding in the Methodist ministry. A record of the proceedings of Holston Conference for the year 1888 carries a memoir of Rev. John S. Bourne. It recites that "he was converted at Ebenezer, Jan. 17, 1875, at a revival conducted by the eccentric and notable Bob Sheffey."

In reading this manuscript to Dr. E. E. Wiley, then pastor of the Trinity Methodist church in Bluefield, West Virginia, and for many years a beloved leader in Methodism, it came out in conversation that he was a convert of Rev. John S. Bourne, therefore a spiritual grandson of Robert Sayers Sheffey.

The following stories are recorded in Johnson's "History of the Middle New River Settlements:" "If there was a man beyond any other that believed that the whiskey traffic was one of the devil's strong-holds it was Mr. Sheffey. He assaulted this traffic when opportunity offered and often in public prayed for its overthrow and destruction. He was often appealed to by good people to pray the Lord to remove still-houses and liquor manufacturers. On the upper waters of the Bluestone, many years ago, was a whiskey distillery operated by a man and his son. Mr. Sheffey stopped in the neighborhood at the home of a good Methodist family. The good woman of the house told him of the distillery, and that it was ruining and wrecking the lives of many of the young men in the neighborhood, and requested him to pray for its removal, which he promised to do. The lady inquired 'How long will it be before we may expect our prayers to be answered?' 'About twelve months,' was his reply; and sure enough within the twelve months the distillery was closed up, and the owner and his son in jail on charge of defrauding the government.

"On another occasion he was on Wolf Creek, near Rocky Gap, when he was informed by the mother of a family with whom he was stopping of the existence of a distillery in the neighborhood that was proving a great evil and requested Mr. Sheffey to pray for its removal. Mr. Sheffey then and there went to the Lord in prayer, and asked Him to destroy the evil, and if necessary send fire from Heaven to burn it up, and that very night an old tree near the distillery took fire, fell on the shanty and destroyed the whole thing. The whole neighborhood firmly believed Sheffey's prayer brought down that fire, which rid the neighborhood of the evil.

"As has already been stated, Mr. Sheffey went to the Lord about everything he did, even about small things, which sometimes brought him into ridicule by some classes of people, but that did not in the least deter him. He believed that the Lord controlled the actions of animals as well as men, and its verification and illustration thereof the following story is told by a gentleman living a few miles south of Pearisburg, Virginia. Mr. Sheffey stopped at his house over night, and by Mr. Sheffey's direction his horse was turned on pasture. Mr. Sheffey having an appointment for the next day, and anxious to get off early requested the gentleman to have his horse ready for him. The man went out very early to get the horse which he was unable to do, even summoning help, still the horse would not allow himself to be caught, nor would he be driven into the stable yard or lot. Finally the man gave up the effort to secure the horse, went to the house and informed Mr. Sheffey of the situation, and he went out with the man into the field where the horse was grazing, and requested the man to wait until he told the Lord about it. Down upon his knees he went and told the Lord of the inability of the man to bridle the horse and requested that He put it into the mind of the horse to stand and be bridled, and on rising from his knees he said to the man 'You can now bridle the horse,' which he immediately did. Many other things like this occurred in the history of this man; there is just one other incident of his life which will be related, as it shows that he was a man whose religion was pure and undefiled and near akin to that of our blessed Saviour. Mr. Sheffey's hostility and open expressions against liquor traffic and the traffickers, often brought down upon him, not only the curses and imprecations of these people, but once at least, a pounding upon his head. He was preaching in Bland county, and during the service was interrupted by some unthoughted young men under the influence of ardent spirits, which led to their severe censure and arraignment by the preacher, which so offended and enraged them that they took position at the outside of the church door, and as Mr. Sheffey went out they clubbed and beat him severely. These people were indicted in the Court of Bland county, and Mr. Sheffey summoned as a witness for the Commonwealth. He did not appear, and compulsory process was taken against him, and on his appearance in Court he endeavored to avoid testifying. The young men were convicted, when Mr. Sheffey with tears in his eyes, and a prayer on his lips implored the court to allow them to go unpunished, that they knew not what they did; that he had forgiven them, that he had asked the Lord to forgive them, and now asked the court to forgive them, which in a measure it did. Whatever may be said of this peculiar man and his eccentricities, his like will never be seen again. He died in peace with God and man, and all who knew him revere his memory."

The incident herein recited with reference to the abuse of Sheffey by two toughs occurred at the home of Josiah Bruce in the eastern end of Bland county, according to James R. Bogle, who at the age of eighty years, resided on Wythe Avenue in Bluefield, W. Va. He said that Sheffey would visit at the home of his grandmother, Peggy Bogle, also at Rhoda Helvey's and Josiah Bruce. While here he would preach. One evening he preached at Bruce's home and made mention of a distillery in the community which was wrecking the lives of many people in the neighborhood, etc. Three young men were there who became very much incensed at his remarks. After the service Sheffey stepped out into the yard and two of these men attacked him with their fists and pummeled him unmercifully. He cried out until some of those on the inside rushed out to rescue him from the hands of his attackers.

The men made their escape and fled to the west. They were indicted in the courts of Bland county. It was during the trial that Sheffey begged for mercy for the culprit who had returned to Bland county after a few years in the west. He was allowed to go after paying a fine for his offense, said fine being paid by the grandfather of this man. He lived only a few brief years afterwards. The other man never returned to Bland county, dying in the west a few years later. This incident, according to Mr. Bogle, took place, about the year 1868 or 1870. In the Bogle home one sees a very fine picture of Brother Sheffey, the gift of his son, "Eddie."

The Bristol News of February 18, 1890, published a sermon prepared by the Rev. B. F. White on "The Method to Defeat the Institutions of Intemperance" in the course of which he recites these incidents in which Brother Sheffey played a very prominent part. It follows:

"In the year 1855, we were on the Wytheville circuit. We found R. S. Sheffey, who had been trying to get license to preach for several years and failed, because he was a peculiar man. We succeeded in having him licensed to preach and then kept him with us for three years. He spends about two-thirds of his waking hours in prayer. His prayers are very frequently answered immediately! And in nothing more frequently than for the downfall of establishments for intemperance. We were riding by a distillery, he said, 'Let's you and I pray against this still house." We agreed. He said, 'Hold my horse until I go in and pray with the family,' but they would not let him pray, as we told him. A widow lady was the proprietor. She took sick and died in a very short time; leaving a son to succeed her. He became insane and was sent to an asylum. The place was sold, and the distillery ended at the place, all too, in a very short time!

"On another creek there were three distilleries. We preached this same text, ('And all things whatsoever ye shall ask in prayer believing ye shall receive it.'—Matt. 21:22.), and gave due notice of our agreement to pray for the downfall of the distilleries! The proprietor of the one on the lower end, was a well-to-do man, with robust health. Brother Sheffey prayed that his still might be prized out with a crow-bar. The proprietor died very suddenly and the administrators were actually prizing the still out with a crow-bar before they thought of Sheffey's prayer.

"The proprietor of the one above this was an old man. Brother Sheffey prayed that his still house might be turned into a sheep-pen. In a very short time he sold his farm to a good Methodist, and a Christian family, who actually made a sheep-pen out of the still house.

"The proprietor of the upper one was a very wicked man, who, when he found out we were praying for the downfall of his still house threatened to whip us, and actually made the attempt! Brother Sheffey prayed that a tree might fall on his still house and break its back! The people were surprised at the prayer as there was no tree near the place, but in a short time a great storm came and actually landed a tree on the still house.

"Across the mountain from there was a large steam distillery. Brother Sheffey expostulated with the proprietors, but they treated him with contempt. He spent the whole night in prayer for its downfall. In three days the whole establishment was consumed by fire.

"We have never known his prayers to fail of being answered on such occasions. We have known his prayers answered immediately, in numbers of instances."

Rev. White adds: "Let an individual Christian, like Brother Sheffey free himself from all things offensive to God, and then challenge the supporters of intemperance to a test of prayer; and as sure as the sun shines in the heavens God will establish the truth of His word, by an answer to prayer in such a way that will blacken the defiant face of the institutions of intemperance, until they shall become a hissing, and a by-word in the land; and until the wrath of man shall praise the Lord."

The following appeared in the Richmond Christian Advocate edited by Dr. John J. Lafferty in the year 1888: "A few years ago we gave in an editorial letter a description of a famous character in Southwester Virginia—'Bob' Sheffey. He is an eccentric man of great piety, held in admiration and love by the people, and feared especially by distillers. He prays in public and by name against the stillhouses. It is well authenticated that his prayers have been answered to the destruction of such dens of the devil. He besought God that a tree might fall upon a certain one and that the foundation might be removed and used for a better building. Sure enough, an oak mashed the roof, and after a time the rocks were carried away and made the substructure of a barn. Whiskey men fled away from a certain creek for fear of his prayers.

"A curious matter occurred on Cripple Creek. The new railroad put up a water-tank. Sheffey saw it thought it a big 'mash tub' for whiskey. He publicly prayed it might go to pieces. It is well authenticated that next morning the tank was in fragments."

Quoting again from Johnson's "History of the Middle New River Settlements and Contiguous Territory" we got these incidents from the life of Brother Sheffey: "At a meeting held by Mr. Sheffey at Jordan's Chapel, now in Summers county, Dr. Bray, a physician in the neighborhood, together with his wife, was present at a Sunday morning service and had with them a nursing infant child, which was taken suddenly ill about the close of the service. The mother became alarmed and grief-stricken about the condition of her child, and in her paroxysms she cried out that her child was dying. A large number of people were present and gathered around the mother and child supposed to be dying, when Mr. Sheffey appeared and being informed of the cause of the trouble, said, 'Brother, give me the little child,' and taking it in his arms he fell upon his knees, and in a most earnest prayer to God asked for the life of the little child and that it might be restored to its mother. Arising from his position on the ground, he handed the child to its father, remarking, 'Here, brother, is your little child well and all right;' and so it was.

"Mr. Sheffey had a right good vein of humor in his make-up, and he occasionally exercised that faculty to the discomfiture of people. Some thirty years ago, there lived on the upper waters of Brush Creek, a Christian gentleman by the name of Robert Karr, a member of the Methodist church, at whose house Mr. Sheffey was entertained, when on his preaching tours in that neighborhood. He had a protracted service in the neighborhood of Mr. Karr, which had continued some weeks, and which Mr. Karr had not attended, and whose non-attendance Mr. Sheffey had observed, and taking his brother Karr to task about the matter of his lack of interest in the meeting, inquired why he did not attend; Mr. Karr replied that he had a good reason, and being pressed by Mr. Sheffey to give his reason, he finally said, 'Well, I don't just exactly like your way'; whereupon Mr. Sheffey said with a ha! ha! 'Neither does the devil.'

"On the occasion last mentioned or a similar one, while Mr. Sheffey was holding a meeting at Mr. Karr's early one Sunday morning, a young man rode up to the house and delivered to Mr. Sheffey a message from his wife that his little son, Eddie, was very sick, and that the doctors had said he could not live and for him to come home at once. Mr. Sheffey made no response to the message, but went off a distance to some high granite boulders on the top of the highest of which he went to the Lord in prayer, and continued to pray until the time had arrived for him to meet his congregation at the church. On reaching the pulpit, he related to his congregation the message he had received, and then said, 'I have talked to the Lord about this, and Eddie is not going to die.' Eddie still lives, a bright, intelligent, useful and honored citizen.

"Mr. Sheffey had wonderful faith in God's providences, his care for his people in providing for their wants, physical as well as spiritual. It is told of him that on one occasion he met a man in the road on a very cold day, and that the man had on no socks, and that Mr. Sheffey observing this took off his and gave them to the man. After riding some distance he stopped at a house to warm his feet, and the lady of the house said to him that she had knit for him a nice pair of socks which she wished to present him. Another thing may be mentioned of this man, and that was the tender care of his horse and of other animals. He could not bear to see them suffer, not even a bug if turned on its back, and he has been known to dismount from his horse and turn it over. If he found what appeared to him to be a hungry animal or dog, he would give it his lunch rather than eat it himself. The story is told of him and another preacher who were out in the wild mountain district, that on leaving the house where they had been entertained, the woman put a lunch in Mr. Sheffey's saddle-bags telling them that they were not likely to meet with their dinner, that day, and that she had provided a lunch that they might not suffer hunger. Off the preachers went on along the mountain pathway during the morning hours and until about noon, when Mr. Sheffey's companion who being in front halted, and proposed to eat the lunch. Mr. Sheffey informed him that he had no lunch, that he had just met two very hungry looking dogs to which he had given the lunch."

I herewith append an article written by Rev. Charles A. Brown of Narrows, Virginia, on Sheffey. This was written for the author by Rev. Brown who has since died. Rev. Brown was an outstanding educator, minister, and business man, during his active life. At the time he wrote the article he was eighty-two years old and an active member of the Narrows Methodist church. While I was the pastor there an enlarged picture of Brother Brown was presented to the church by a group of admirers in recognition of the long years of service rendered the organization in Christian endeavor. This picture was hanged in the church auditorium. The sketch follows:

ROBERT SHEFFEY

The following article consists of some recollections and observations made on the life of Robert Sheffey, adhering to what I know from personal contacts with him.

My first acquaintance with him began about 70 years ago when I was a mere boy. Sheffey, on one of his evangelistic tours, stopped at my parent's home on Wolfe Creek to get his dinner and his horse fed. He at that time impressed me with one of his peculiar traits of character. While eating dinner his horse got loose in the field, and when Sheffey undertook to catch him he would run and play about in the field. I helped try to hem the horse which we could not do. Sheffey said to me, "Let us leave him alone until I pray to the Lord about it." He bowed down and prayed some length of time after which he again attempted to bridle the horse, but the animal still refused to be caught for a while. Finally he gave up and was bridled. This was very amusing to me as I had never seen a horse caught that way before.

Sheffey's Circuit

Sheffey's circuit or evangelistic rounds in those days consisted of Giles county and parts of Mercer and Bland counties. He appeared to make some three or four tours on his charge each year, being away from home probably a month at a time. His traveling outfit consisted of a good horse, saddle, saddle bags, sheep-skin, and necessary articles of clothing. He lived among the people with little thought of remuneration, depending upon such gifts as the people were disposed to give him. He seemed to have little concern for his family, evidently leaving the care of his family to Providence.

Sheffey's Peculiarities

Sheffey was in many respects a unique character. He had oddities that made him appear eccentric; though such a condition might be expected of any man so deeply absorbed in religious matters as Sheffey was. His whole time and thought were centered upon one subject, that of religion. He was a man of one Book, the Bible, and of one purpose, that of consecration to God. He was a man of great faith and had the courage of an honest conviction. A large part of his time was taken up in prayer and shouting. He sought secluded places where he could commune with God undisturbed. He had a thorough knowledge of the Scriptures and could quote them readily and with telling effect.

Sheffey's Personality

Sheffey in personal appearance showed culture and was very polite and modest, with a saintly look, only fairly well dressed, neat and very clean in his habits. In the homes of the people he was at times critical as to conditions about the home. If things were not orderly he would call attention to them. He preached cleanliness. If the towels and bedding were not clean he would say something about them, and suggest soap and water. Sometimes in the pulpit he would call attention to how he had been treated. At the table he would ask for things not on the table. He had a tooth for sweet things, especially honey and sugar. On one occasion in eating at my mother's table he gave her a gentle hint as to what he had received on a previous visit. He said, "When I was here before you gave me something, the name of which sounded like backwall." Mother answered, "O, I see; what you want is jam." Sheffey got the blackberry jam. If Sheffey had a fault it was his disposition to gratify an inordinate appetite.

Sheffey made a deep impression in family worship. Everything had to be carried out in first-class order. The outside members of the family must be called together, after which he would quote Scripture, probably an entire chapter. This was followed by a familiar hymn, and then a long prayer of spiritual fervor.

Sheffey As A Preacher

Sheffey could not be called a good preacher. He had a style peculiar to himself. He would take a text at the outset, and probably never return to it. His preaching consisted largely of giving his experience of what he had seen and heard in his travels mingling with the people. He at times would preach at great length, an hour or more, and would become tedious to listen to. His main strength was in his prayer and spiritual power. His manner of conducting a service was of the old-time Methodist order. He was a great believer in the altar, no hand-shaking process would answer the purpose in a conversion. Penitents must be kept at the altar until soundly converted, and could testify to the same.

I have a vivid recollection of one of the great meetings held at the First Methodist Church in Narrows. Great spiritual power was manifested. People were being converted in large numbers. The whole church seemed to be moved.

A rather amusing thing took place at this meeting while some people were working in the congregation and others working at the altar. Shouting was going on, and someone knocked down a long stove-pipe, all of which had but little effect on the meeting. The shouting continued till a late hour at night.

Sheffey on coming into the community directed his attention first to the closing out of the bar-rooms, believing nothing could be accomplished until the whiskey men could be gotten out. The bar-keeper would close out his business. On one occasion he professed religion and came into the revival and worked with penitents.

Sheffey during his long period as a local evangelist had a large following. But few are left at this time to do him honor and perpetuate his name. "He being dead, yet speaketh."—(End of Article.)

It is an interesting observation to make that the author of the above article dates the beginning of his long Christian experience to the ministry of Robert Sayers Sheffey.

Chapter VII

More Stories About Sheffey

Shortly after the death of Brother Sheffey, in 1902, an article was published in a Wythe county paper which tells the following story: "People still living recall that on one occasion a new still house was being constructed on Wolf Creek when Mr. Sheffey came along on his horse, and observed the men at work on the building. He dismounted and on bended knee asked the Lord to destroy the thing. In a short time a large oak tree blew down and mashed the still house into smithereens. The promoter of the enterprise began the erection of another still house with the result that the famous preacher passed the spot again, and when he saw what was taking place he again dismounted and sent up a fervent prayer for the destruction of the building. Within less than a week a terrific flood visited the section and washed away the new still house, not leaving a board."

This story came from Robert Sheffey, the grandson. It is recorded just as he furnished it to the writer in these words: "Judge Bernard Mason, of Pearisburg, recounted to me a unique story several years ago. My Grandfather loved to write and to draw pictures of birds and fish, and sometimes he would make these pictorial and piscatorial designs. His hand-writing was very interesting and individual. Judge Mason said it is told that one day as the minister was riding horseback along the road he came to a large flat, shelving rock. This, he thought, offered an excellent place for an inscription and he dismounted and inscribed upon the exposed surface of the rock in large legible letters these words: 'What shall I do to be saved?' He then went on. Not long afterwards, a patent medicine salesman happened that way and read the inscription upon the rock. He added underneath the inscription this: 'Use Hite's Pain Cure.' Again, it is said, Brother Sheffey returned to the spot and in passing there saw what had happened and he then added a further inscription under the preceding: 'And prepare to meet thy God.' "

Rev. George A. Maiden, former district superintendent

and for more than 50 years an honored member of the Holston conference, said that a revival was in progress at the Forest church, near Ivanhoe, Wythe county, Virginia. Brother Sheffey had been present at most of the services, but the ministers in charge of the services had paid but scant attention to him. This rather irked him, but he said nothing about it. The meeting had made no progress and finally those in charge decided that they would ask Brother Sheffey to offer the prayer at the next service. Up to this time Sheffey had not been called upon to pray, for "the brethren" feared that he might pray too long. Sheffey opened his prayer in words which were about as follows: "O Lord, Thou knowest that this Thy servant has been here all these days, and those here have never recognized him as Thy servant, and, now Lord, I don't know what Thou thinkest of them, but as for me I think they are small potatoes and few in the hill."

Rev. James R. Brown, for forty-two years a member of the Holston Conference, tells how Brother Sheffey used to visit the home of his father, John R. Brown, in Tazewell county, when he was a young lad. One day while in the home he laid his hand on the head of the boy and prayed that God "might make a preacher out of him, and that he might live to see a thousand souls brought into the Kingdom." Across the years Brother Brown has kept a record of those who have been converted under his ministry and to his very great surprise when he had totaled them up they reached the thousandth mark. Strange were his prayers, and strange were the answers! But the important thing to remember is that the answers came in due time.

Attorney James Kahle, of Bluefield, W. Va., told this story to Robert A. Sheffey, grandson of Brother Sheffey. The old preacher stopped in the home of Mr. Kahle's parents one day for dinner. When they were seated at the dinner table and someone began to look for a butter knife, Mrs. Kahle, in a very apologetic manner, remarked that she could not find the butter knife. Brother Sheffey, in a very affable manner, answered, "That's all right, Sister Kahle, the Lord will provide a butter knife." The incident was forgotten, and long months afterward Mr. Kahle had occasion to go to Baltimore to attend to a business matter. While there he thought how nice it would be to bring some needed gift to his wife. He dropped into a store and what should he buy but a butter knife? He told how he had forgotten what Brother Sheffey had said, but there was the butter knife!

Brother Sheffey had been away on a "preaching tour" and at the conclusion of his work he returned to Staffordsville where he lived. Shortly before he reached the home someone met him, and told him that Mr. So-and-So was critically ill, and that the family would like to have him come and pray with him before he died. All unmindful of the fact that he was almost within sight of home, he rode over to the neighbor's and prayed for the sick man. Suddenly turning to the man who had brought him the message concerning the sick man, he said, "By-the-way, how's Mrs. Sheffey?"

One day Brother Sheffey said to his son, "Eddy, plenty of water inside and out is the best thing for anybody."

Rev. G. T. Jordan, retired Methodist pastor, was a former pastor of the Mechanicsburg charge, in Bland county, and knew Brother Sheffey. He also knew many of the characters who had known Brother Sheffey in the incidents which he relates and testifies to the accurateness of the stories herein recited.

At the Redoak church on the Ceres charge, in Bland county, Brother Sheffey was holding a meeting. The enthusiasm was dull and the preacher became very much concerned about its success. Someone who happened to be passing along the road saw Brother Sheffey kneeling in prayer in front of the church at a time not appointed for service. At the appointed hour, and at the beginning of the service, there came tumbling through the ceiling an object which had the appearance of a huge stone. It struck the floor and rolled down the aisle to a double door which seemed to open of its own accord, and then rolled out into the yard. This created quite a bit of excitement, but Brother Sheffey appeared to be perfectly calm. He turned to someone and requested that they go look and see if his horse was still standing where he had tethered the animal. Then he remarked: "Brethren, I told you that the Lord was going to shake up this place." A man who was present at this service related the incident to Brother Jordan. What about the revival? A great meeting came to the community.

At Mechanicsburg, in Bland county, there stands a Christian church on a spot where a distillery had formerly stood. Brother Sheffey prayed for the removal of the distillery, and that a church might be erected on the site. And it so happened.

Near Slate Springs, in Wythe county, there stands a beautiful country church close by the spot where there was once a distillery. Brother Sheffey was riding along one day and met a man coming from the still with a jug of whiskey. Whereupon the preacher dismounted, got down on his knees, and prayed for the destruction of the still, and that a church be erected at that place. His prayer was answered.

At Spratt's Creek, in Smyth county, Virginia, there was a distillery. Brother Sheffey prayed that it might be removed, and that a hog-pen take its place. Again his prayer was answered.

At Asbury, on the head-waters of Cripple Creek, in Wythe county, Brother Sheffey was being entertained in a certain home. At the conclusion of a meal he filled his mouth with sugar syrup and went out into the sugar maple grove to pray and praise God. He got very happy and put his arms, as far as they would reach, around what he thought was a sugar tree. While he was praying a buckeye fell, striking him on the head. He looked up and exclaimed, "Lord, I was mistaken; I thought it was a sugar tree but it's a buckeye."

Near Oakvale he went out into a woodland to pray and while upon his knees a very fierce dog came toward him in a menacing way. Brother Sheffey, discovering the dog, sprang to his feet and ran to a nearby spring-house. He sprang upon the roof, but it would not support his weight. He fell through the roof and striking the ground he exclaimed, "Thank God for spring-houses."

In the East end of Bland county there lived a young husband and wife who became estranged for some reason. They separated. Brother Sheffey heard of the trouble and visited in the home of a relative of these young persons. He spent the most of the afternoon in prayer to the end that they might be re-united. Late in the afternoon he came out of the parlor rejoicing and told the family that the couple would soon be brought together again. That very evening they were re-united and have lived happily together ever since. Brother Jordan who tells this story knew the couple personally and in speaking of this happening recites that they are very fine characters.

Brother Sheffey and the late Rev. Charles W. Kelley were making their way down the southside of Big Walker mountain, near Mechanicsburg, in Bland county, one wintry day. The mountain-side was coated with ice and the path was very steep. They were leading their horses because of the hazardous condition of the path they were taking down the mountainside. Brother Sheffey's horse slipped and fell at the very brink of the abrupt cliff or precipice. He called upon Brother Kelley to hold the bridle of his horse to keep him from going over while he prayed. The horse slipped over the embankment but received no injury whatever. Brother Kelley told this story quite often in talking of his experiences with Brother Sheffey.

On Wolf Creek, just below Rocky Gap post-office, in Bland county, there was a very treacherous ford. Very often the ford would fill with quick-sand making it dangerous for horses and cattle to cross. This had been so for a long time. Brother Sheffey knew of the dread of the people who had to cross the stream at this ford. One evening he prayed at the Rocky Gap Methodist church: "Lord, send a freshet and fill this treacherous ford with sand so hard that a cow's hoof will not dent it." That very thing happened and the ford remains safe until this day. Dr. Bogle who was a practicing physician at Rocky Gap at the time of the happening recited the story to Rev. Jordan.

There lived in the East end of Smyth county, near Chatham Hill, a very prominent family. The husband became very angry with Brother Sheffey because he did not approve of his prayers. This man's wife became critically ill and Brother Sheffey heard of the illness. He learned that the doctors had despaired of her recovery. But this fact did not hinder him in his prayers. He went into the woods in the same community where the family resided and spent several hours praying for the recovery of the woman. Late in the evening he came out of the woods shouting and went to a nearby home telling them to "Go tell Brother W. that Sister W. is going to get well." And she did.

There's a home in the Eastern end of Bland county, known after the death of her husband, as "Aunt Julia Bogle's home." This was also known as "the preacher's home." Brother Sheffey was as much inclined to visit this home as was Jesus to visit the home of Lazarus in Bethany. On one occasion while he was visiting there, and after dinner had been served, he requested John Bogle, "Aunt Julia's son," to go down into the meadow and catch his horse and saddle him, for he wanted to be on his way. John went, but the horse would romp and play, and he was unable to get a bridle over his head. John's sister saw what was happening and she went and told Brother Sheffey. The preacher went out of the house, and into the chimney corner, and knelt down to pray that the horse might stand still until the young man had caught him. John had seen Brother Sheffey go into the chimney corner and he knew what was taking place. He picked up the bridle again and walked up to the horse which stood perfectly still until the bridle was over his head.

At Mt. Zion church, in the Eastern end of Bland county, Brother Sheffey had an appointment to preach. When he got up to begin the service he said: "Brethren, if any of you have the headache I have a recipe for you." Whereupon a certain brother who was suffering with a severe headache held up his hand at the request of the preacher. Brother Sheffey said: "Brother, get a towel and some soap and go down to the creek and take a good bath." The vein of humour that seemed to run through his body and soul would at times give expression to itself in the most unheard of manner.

At an altar service, in the Wabash camp-meeting, there was a young lady at the mourner's bench in whom Brother Sheffey was very much interested. She was deeply penitent, and, as she cried out of a broken heart, Brother Sheffey began to sing, "Old Satan's mad, and I am glad; he's lost a soul he thought he had." The refrain ran, "Bless the Lord, I'm happy on the way." This at the end of each line.

And the chorus: "Happy on the way; happy on the way; bless the Lord, I'm happy on the way."

A certain intellectual and cultured D. D. from the Baltimore conference was not pleased with Brother Sheffey's style of singing and shouted out: "Sing something else, brethren; sing something else." Brother Sheffey continued: "I see the brother doesn't like my song, but for the life of me, I see nothing wrong with it." And here he started out with the refrain again. Then the good brother called out again, "Sing something else, brethren; sing something else. Sing 'Jesus Lover of My Soul.'"

Just at this point the young lady was very happily converted. She arose shouting the praises of God. The disturbed brother from Baltimore being near the spot where the young lady was shouting, Brother Sheffey looked at him and said, "Brother, stand back and let the sister shout."

George W. Lucado, for many years the agent of the Norfolk & Western railway, located at Ada, W. Va., recites a number of interesting stories about Brother Sheffey. He knew the old preacher when he was a lad, and has many interesting recollections of his visits to the Lucado home on Wolf Creek. He says: "I remember several things about him. He was no great preacher, but most powerful in prayer. He loved, and would pray for everybody and everything that God permitted to exist. He never failed to pray for the honey bees saying, 'Lord, bless the little honey bees for they make sweet honey. Like Sweet Jesus'. He would often visit the home of my wife's grandmother, Mrs. Sarah Ann Maxwell, on Wolf Creek, near the Green Valley church. Near this home stood a chestnut tree, and grandmother would always have honey with her meals, and after Brother Sheffey was through eating he would fill his mouth with honey, make straight for this tree, climb it, and shout, until all the honey had melted."

Mr. Lucado said he heard Brother Sheffey preach on divorce one night at the Eggleston Methodist church. It so happened that a lady was present who had just been divorced, and she was going with a Mr. Charlie C_____, a very fine man and the choir leader. And imagine the embarrassment of this couple when Brother Sheffey said, about divorced women; I wouldn't have one of them. When I get one I want a fresh one."

The following story was told by his mother, writes Mr Lucado, in the presence of a young lady who was a first cousin to the man involved in the incident. The young man's name was "Bill" S_____. He was a wild wicked youngster. One day, while rolling logs in a new-ground, he was caught by one of the larger logs and badly crushed through the body. Brother Sheffey was called to pray with him and his prayer ran something like this: 'Lord, be merciful to this young man. Let him live until he can repent of his sins and be baptized, and then if he does not intend to live right, take him out of the way of the other young people of this community." The youth lived for two weeks, was baptized in New River, near Burton, Va., and then went home and took to his bed and died in a very short time.

Another story from Brother Lucado: "Brother Sheffey came to our home one day and remained for dinner. Mother was busy preparing the meal, and he said to me, 'Sonny, get me a glass of water.' I did; he drank a sup of it and bathed his face with the remainder. Within a few minutes he asked for a second and a third glass of water and used them the same way. Boy-like, I wanted to ask him why he washed so much, but I was afraid that mother would hear me, and I knew what that would mean if she did. A short time later mother had to go out to the spring-house for some milk and butter. About this time Brother Sheffey asked for the fourth glass. Seeing I was in the clear, I said, 'Brother Sheffey, why do you wash so much?' He answered, 'O Sonny, Jesus says you must keep clean,' and I asked him no more questions.

It is told that Brother Sheffey was riding through Tazewell county, Virginia, and became quite hungry. He got off his horse, walked over into a fence corner and knelt upon his sheep-skin. He asked God to direct him to some place where he could get dinner. After he had prayed, he climbed back on his horse, and, after passing a number of nice looking homes, he came to a very humble looking log house. He stopped, tied his horse to the gate, and walked toward the house. To his surprise, perhaps, an old colored woman peeped out of the window, and said, "Lordy mercy,

Brudder Sheffey, de good Lord done told me dat you would be here for dinner, and I has gone and killed you a chicken."

George Johnson, who lives near Trigg postoffice, in Giles county, said that Brother Sheffey was a visitor in the home of his parents quite often when he was a youth. He said the preacher stopped one day for dinner. While in the home he saw two of the Johnson boys pick up their guns and start out to hunt rabbits. Brother Sheffey said to Mrs. Johnson, the mother, "Where are the boys going?" The mother advised that they were going for a hunt. The preacher said, "The sweet little conies (rabbits); they ought not be killed." The boys went on, jumped the rabbits, but they were unable to kill a single one. This was unusual for the Johnson boys to return without their game, but they couldn't hit a single one that day. When they returned, Brother Sheffey said to Mrs. Johnson, "Did the boys get any game?" And she answered, "No." The preacher smiled and said, "I thought so."

Mr. Johnson said that he had seen Mr. Sheffey get off his horse at a certain rock, pointed out to us, and pray before he started across the Big Ridge which fronted the Johnson home. The road left Whitney's branch, near the Trigg postoffice, and ran parallel with the Big Ridge for a half mile or more where it intersected with the Bane road. Sheffey traveled this road a great deal, but according to Mr. Johnson, he never crossed the ridge until he knelt at this rock and prayed. Is it any wonder that he made his journeys through this mountainous country which had nothing but trails for roads, and that he traveled in perfect safety?

Robert A. Sheffey, the Bluefield architect and grandson of Brother Sheffey, tells the following story which was given to him by the late Thomas Lee Felts, member of the Baldwin-Felts Detective Agency, and resident of Galax and Bluefield. The detective recalled that in a certain section many years ago the people were experiencing a great drouth. There had been no rain for weeks. The earth was parching with dry heat and vegetation was terribly scorched. The people called upon Brother Sheffey to pray for rain. Mr. Felts said the minister lifted up his voice and prayed: "O Lord, send us rain; send us rain in abundance. Do not just give us a light shower, but let us have a 'clod-buster' and a 'gully-washer.'" It is said that that very night the rains descended in torrents and nearly washed everything away.

Robert Sheffey says that his father, Edward F. Sheffey, once told him that on a bitter cold day as his grandfather was riding along on his itinerary he met a man who was in his shirt sleeves and who had no coat and was suffering from the cold. The preacher immediately removed his own coat and proffered it to the unfortunate individual. The man did not like to accept. It is related that Brother Sheffey then said: "That's all right, brother; I want you to have it; the Lord will provide another for me." And the grandson adds: "I do not believe that the Lord or his friends ever failed him at any time."

Alex. St. Clair, a prominent citizen of Tazewell county and large land-owner and farmer of St. Clair's crossing, near Bluefield, Virginia, prior to his death some years ago recited many stories that had come to him. Some of these happenings came under the observation of Mr. St. Clair for his home was a favorite stopping place for the preacher. Dr. Charles T. St. Clair, Sr., a prominent citizen and eye, ear, nose and throat specialist, of Bluefield, W. Va., told us that he once heard his father tell how he had heard Brother Sheffey pray as follows: "Our dear, kind, sweet, benevolent Heavenly Father, may we be permitted when we reach sweet Heaven to dive down into the sea of glory and pop up about forty yards from where we went down and light on the 'Tree of Life,' and shake the silvery drops from our golden wings, if we have any, O Lord."

The doctor says that the last time he saw Brother Sheffey he spent the night at his father's home. After a lengthy prayer in which he prayed for his lame horse, the doctor said that he recalled that he was showing the preacher upstairs to his room. He turned and said to Mrs. St. Clair, "Sister, do your prettiest tomorrow morning." The good woman did not understand so he said again, "Sister, do your prettiest for breakfast in the morning."

It was not unusual for Brother Sheffey to drop an open hint to his hostess to have chicken and dumplings at the meal. One day a good sister invited him to dinner with her family the next day. In response to the kind invitation he replied: "Don't put yourself to any trouble, sister, but if you have chicken, please have dumplings." It is a safe guess that Brother Sheffey was just like the average Methodist preacher—he "loved" fried chicken, but he probably 'loved' boiled chicken and dumplings almost as well as fried chicken.

Brother Sheffey visited his son at Lynchburg upon one occasion and as he traveled by train he met some men. He wrote a letter to some friends back in Giles county in which he told of this chance acquaintance. He said, in the letter, "One was converted at my meeting near Snowville or some place, and he got back, but he became religious the second time and was trying to hold on. He said he was present when I prayed for the downfall of Mr. M_____ still house, and the Lord sent a snow and mashed the roof in and he wound up his stilling, and one of his sons got to preaching, or trying to get ready to preach, and I spared him two dollars to help him to prepare at school for the ministry. I think he got license to preach and started out as a preacher. May God help him!"

In a conversation with Judge Bernard Mason, an estimable citizen of Pearisburg, Virginia, he told the writer of having visited the old Wabash camp meeting where he heard Brother Sheffey pray at one of the services. He said the prayer must have been at least an hour long. Brother Sheffey prayed for everything that he could think of that was worthy of prayer. He also mentioned a number of persons by name in his prayer. Among other things the old saint said in his prayer, and a thing that made a very profound impression upon the lawyer's mind was this: "O Lord, make this world a little heaven to go to big heaven in." The judge said he had never forgotten those words. At this same time there was a man by the name of Pickle at the altar seeking the forgiveness of his sins. And Brother Sheffey remembered him in his prayer in these words: "O Lord, bless Brother Pickle, and may his heart not be so sour as his name."

The home of W. Newton Mustard, near Newberry's Chapel, in Bland county, was a favorite stopping place with Brother Sheffey. Robert Mustard, a son of Newton Mustard, a resident of Narrows, Va., said that the preacher came to his father's house and spent a day upon one occasion. There was a very excellent spring near the Mustard home and Brother Sheffey drank a great deal of water. He kept calling for water and Robert Mustard, then a small lad, was kept busy carrying the pitcher to and from the spring. As he told the story, after the eleventh trip, young Mustard conceived the idea of bringing a bucket of water to the house and placing it on the porch near the door. When Brother Sheffey would call for more water he would take the pitcher out on the porch and fill it up. He did this for a number of times and Brother Sheffey would always say, after smacking his lips, 'Sonny, the water is fine." He always thought that the water came from the spring. Mr. Mustard said that he filled the glass up sixteen times during the day with which to quench the thirst of the preacher.

Robert Mustard said that he had known Brother Sheffey to pray for at least three or four hours in his devotions. He relates how he had overheard him as he walked around or sat in his chair talking with God as if He were some friend sitting beside him. He said that his mother used to put honey in a dish for the preacher and he would take it with him to his room. Here he would fill his mouth with the honey saying that it would sweeten his mouth so that "he could talk to the Lord better then." One day he had his mouth filled with honey and boy-like, Mustard said, "Brother Sheffey, it looks like you would swallow the honey." Before he could think, the old fellow swallowed the honey and said, "There now, I didn't want to swallow it yet; I wanted to talk some more with the Lord."

Another interesting story of how "the prayer of a righteous man availeth much" is related by Rev. Z. D. Holbrook, member of the Holston Conference since 1902. This incident came under Brother Holbrook's own observation because it happened at the home of his father, "Uncle Jimmy" Holbrook, a local preacher in the Methodist whose home was in Wright's Valley, near the Bailey church on the Graham circuit. Mrs. Holbrook had a turkey hen that wanted to "set." She lacked two eggs having enough to "set" the hen so she decided that she would place two goose eggs along with the turkey eggs making a full "setting." This she did. All were hatched and the whole brood was growing nicely. One night an old fox came along and caught the turkey hen and after killing her carried her off above the barn. Brother Sheffey happened by about this time and stopped at the Holbrook home where he was always a welcome guest, its doors ever open to the "man of God." Mrs. Holbrook related the happenings to the preacher and that night when family prayers were in order the whole burden of Brother Sheffey's prayer was that God might put it into the heart of the gobbler, the head of the turkey gang, to "mother" the little turkeys and goslings until they were able to take care of themselves. Strange as it may seem, this very thing happened. When it rained the male bird took over his job with seeming pride, and the young birds followed him about the yard and across the hills. When they grew older and were able to roost above the ground, the gobbler would fly up on to the roost, the young turkeys would follow him, and then he would fly down on to the ground and try to get the goslings to understand that their places were beside him. He would cut quite a caper because they would not follow out his pleadings, but this, of course, they could not do.

    Mrs. Bowman Stafford, a resident of the White Gate neighborhood, in Giles county, tells a story that seems almost incredible, but the facts came under her personal observation. Mrs. Stafford is a sister of Mr. Aurelius Vest, of White Gate, at whose home Brother Sheffey died. In one of his many journeys Brother Sheffey happened in at a home where the potato bugs were about to destroy the vines and hinder the development of the crop. The potato patch was nearby a piece of ground that was covered with weeds of almost every description. Brother Sheffey heard about the bugs and prayed that God would remedy the situation in some way. Some hours later the good man of the house went down to his potato patch and discovered that the bugs had left the potato vines and moved over into the weed patch and were eating the weeds from the main stem.

    Men and women laugh at these stories, and they are laughable—many of them, but there is an explanation.

Brother Sheffey had faith in God and he talked with God about the commonplace things of life that most of us would not even consider taking to the Lord in prayer. To him, God had to do with everything, large or small, that touches the lives of people. Not a single thing was too insignificant for Him to notice.

Dr. J. A. Baylor, a beloved member of the Holston Conference, now deceased, tells a story which came to him while he was a presiding elder of the Wytheville district. The facts were related to him by someone who knew Brother Sheffey and the other party to the story. The old preacher was visiting at Bland courthouse and had gone into a certain home for a meal. After the meal was over and Brother Sheffey was about ready to go on his way, he said to the good woman of the house, after he had gotten on his horse, "Now, sister, if you will give me a mouthful of that good huckleberry jam I'll be glad." The woman kindly followed out the preacher's suggestion. He put the jam in his mouth and started off down the road towards Mechanicsburg. A short distance down the street an acquaintance who had known Brother Sheffey, and who was known by the preacher, spoke but Sheffey rode on his way apparently unconscious of the fact that anyone had spoken to him. The man was utterly surprised and quite upset. He couldn't understand what had happened. He kept peering toward Sheffey while he kept riding down the street. When Sheffey had gotten to the eastern end of the town where he turned off toward Mechanicsburg he suddenly wheeled his horse around and came riding back to the man. Pulling up his reins he said, "Brother, you will have to excuse me for not speaking; I had my mouth full of huckleberry jam."

G. M. Vandyke, of Tazewell, Virginia, wrote us a letter in which he recorded some Sheffey stories. He said the first service he ever heard him conduct was about the year 1894. At this time he prayed against a distillery on Plum Creek, in Tazewell county. His prayer was to the effect that this distillery might be destroyed and that the place might be converted into a hog pen and then into a barn. Mr. Vandyke adds: "It was destroyed just like he prayed for it to be." Another distillery he prayed against was located near Liberty Hill in the same county. Here he prayed that the distillery might sink into the ground and disappear. "The next morning the distillery was gone. It sank into the earth and the spot is visible from the road."

In 1898 Mr. Vandyke says that he heard him conduct a service at Brushy Hill church in Thompson's Valley, Tazewell county. There was a neighbor, according to Mr. Vandyke, who had a horse that was slowly starving to death because crops were short and the man had no feed with which to take care of the animal. One Sunday in March the horse had gotten down and Mr. Vandyke went over to the man's place and sought to help him with the horse. The man wanted to get the animal into the barn. They failed in their efforts. About this time Sheffey happened along. He saw something was wrong, and, of course, he stopped. He inquired, "What's the trouble?" The man told him that the horse had gotten so thin during the winter because he ran out of hay. The man said he had tried to buy a stack of hay from a neighbor, offering him forty dollars, but the man refused to sell him. Sheffey said to the owner of the horse, "Come on; we will go up to your house and have services." They proceeded to the home and here Sheffey prayed that the horse might get up and into the barn, and that the man who had the hay might be caused to sell it to the man who had sought to buy it at half price." When the service was over, according to Mr. Vandyke, "We looked out and the horse was up and trying to make his way toward the barn. Late that evening the man who had the hay came over and offered the hay to the man saying that he had been thinking the matter over and that he thought twenty dollars was enough for the stack."

The last prayer that Mr. Vandyke heard Sheffey pray was in 1898. In the same county of Tazewell there was a section known as Poor Valley. It was in no sense a poor valley. In fact, it was a very pretty little valley where the people residing therein were quite prosperous. Sheffey didn't like the name so he prayed that the name might be changed. In his prayer he said that "It was too fine a place and too prosperous for such a name." It has been 42 years, says Mr. Vandyke, since I heard him pray this prayer. Recently the name of the valley was changed by the Virginia Legislature to Free Stone Valley.

An interesting letter from Rev. James M. Wysor, one of the most beloved members of the Holston Conference for many years, brings us several new and unheard of stories about Brother Sheffey which we record in these writings as he gave them to us: "Just after the war, my father, George W. Wysor of Dublin, Va., was over on the river near Pearisburg, and spent the night in a farm house where Brother Sheffey was a guest. The next morning, after breakfast, the old man led the family in worship in his characteristic way. After praying for each member of the family, 'the good brother,' and the 'good sister who had fixed the good breakfast,' and the young man, he concluded: 'Now, Lord, I want to pray for your old servant. Lord, your old servant needs a new hat. Lord, put it into the heart of some good brother to give your old servant a new hat. Amen.' It was hard for the young man from bluestocking Presbyterian home to keep from showing some amusement. Starting out for the day, the young man found a loose shoe on his horse, and went to a nearby blacksmith shop. He had to wait for some plow-points to be sharpened, so he hitched the horse, and went back to a store, in front of which he met Brother Sheffey coming out from the farm nearby. A man, coming out of the store, spoke, 'Why hello there, Brother Sheffey. So glad to see you. I haven't seen you since when was the time? Brother Sheffey you need a new hat. Come in here, and he told the merchant to let Brother Sheffey have the best hat in the house. The old man never spoke to his benefactor, but shouted his way back through the store, selected the hat, left the old one on the counter, and shouted his way out. The young man introduced himself to the hat buyer and inquired, 'Did you know that the old gentleman was praying for a hat?' 'No, I didn't know it—didn't know he was in the community; hadn't seen nor heard of him for the past two years'. The hat had been received in about twenty minutes of the request.

"He was a guest of a Mr. Bailey, a Baptist family on Bluestone river, near Spanishburg. After dinner, with his mouth full of honey, he went out into the woods with his sheep-skin for a season of prayer. He got to shouting. Some dogs got after him, and about three big ugly ones were inducing him to move in. Trying to get to the house, the dogs were becoming vicious. His shouting aggravated them, and he climbed a fence, and got on top of a shed roof. Mr. Bailey, working in the hay harvest, came to the rescue, chased the dogs away with his pitchfork, and the old man climbed down shouting, 'Praise the Lord. I have found out what the Baptists are for. They are good to keep the dogs off the Methodists while they shout.'

"The most wonderful story I have heard was his experience near Eggleston or maybe Narrows. Brother Will H. Walker, of the Holston conference told me he knew the facts, first hand. A man who could not make liquor, had a one-eyed man from North Carolina running his still. One night in their revival, Sheffey prayed that the Lord would turn that stillhouse over, or make it into a cow stable; and that one-eyed man that was running the place, that He would convert him, kill him, or send him back to North Carolina where they don't do anything else but make corn liquor. Walker was in the church, and the one-eyed man was outside, at the door, and heard the prayer. Next morning the man demanded his money of the still owner. Not wanting to lose his man, he offered a big raise in salary; but the man said, 'No, I am going.' He said, 'I am not ready to be converted, and I don't want to die, so I am going back to North Carolina, and starting NOW.' The house began to lean over and the owner got locust poles, and propped it that way. Then it began to lean to one end. Same kind of props, and it started the fourth way. The owner got mad and cut all the props and said, 'Let her fall.' A few days later he missed his cows. There had come a deep snow in the night. They looked, listened and inquired. Finally, he told his wife he believed the cows had gone up into the cove before the snow; so he went after them. Just after he started, the wife heard the cows calling for attention, and she found them in the condemned still-house where she milked and fed them. They continued to use the still-house for several years, when they put the cows out, and put in a floor, finished up with chinks and daubing, and rented the house.

"Brother Umberger, old and highly respected citizen at Redoak church, Ceres charge, Bland county, Va., told me that Brother Sheffey was there for a meeting. He had tried for several nights to arouse some interest, and was about to quit discouraged, but announced one more service, "to give the Lord a chance.' That night while he was praying, a very heavy weight fell on the roof of the church, crashed through the roof and ceiling and hit the floor, with an awful jolt, and then rolled from near the front of the house where it struck, back in the aisle and on the right side of the pulpit. It sounded like a full barrel rolling, struck the door which opens in, and burst it 'out' and rolled into the yard. The prayer had stopped, and everyone on foot was looking. The ceiling was not damaged, the roof not hurt, the door, as before, unsplintered, was closed. All looked at each other, then at Brother Sheffey. Sheffey turned to a man, and said, Brother, go out and see if my horse is yet hitched.' The horse was reported 'yet hitched,' and Sheffey proceeded. They had a great meeting.

More than a half century ago the family of Alfred G. Bartlett, a prominent citizen and large land owner, resided at the present site of the town of Fries, Virginia, in Grayson county. Robert Sayers Sheffey was an occasional visitor to this home when he visited in that section. One summer during the haying season the old preacher happened in to spend a few days with the family while engaged in revival work at a nearby church. This was during the haying season and Mr. Bartlett was busily engaged in gathering his crop in the meadows along Stevens Creek. It looked like every day was going to be a rainy day. In fact, the rain clouds were in evidence on every hand and in the afternoons it would rain upon the hills and mountains around the meadows. Mr. Sheffey knew how anxious his host was to gather his crop without the rain falling upon it. In the mornings he would take his sheep-skin with him and make his way across the meadow into a secluded spot where he would spend hours. In the afternoon of the day when the harvesting had ended a heavy rain-storm swept across the meadow. The next morning Brother Sheffey remarked to Mr. Bartlett, "Well, my brother, I see you have your hay up, and it didn't rain upon it." Bartlett replied, "Yes, but it looked like it was going to rain every afternoon." Sheffey answered, "Yes, I know, but I have been praying every day that God would withhold the rain until the haying was finfished." This story was given to us by J. P. Bartlett, a son of Alfred G. Bartlett. He was a small child at the time of the incident but he had heard it from the lips of his father many times.

Now and then, in this modern age, we hear men and women discussing the subject of miracles and asking if the "day of miracles is past." Here is an answer to that question coming from a lady who was healed through the instrumentality of the prayers of Robert Sayers Sheffey. Mrs. C. L. Jarrel, of Rocky Gap, Va., tells of the incident in these words: "I wish to relate a true experience of my own. I was stricken with paralysis in 1895. My face was drawn and I couldn't close my eyes for six weeks. Two doctors had visited me all of that time, but hadn't done me any good. My mother came to see me. She was very much distressed about my condition. She said something had to be done for me. I told her I would not be any better unless Brother Sheffey prayed for me. We didn't know where Brother Sheffey was, but on mother's way home that evening she heard that he was going to preach at Mt. Nebo the following Sunday. She wrote a note and sent to Brother Sheffey by my oldest brother.

"Between 11 and 12 o'clock on Sunday he prayed for me. On the same day I went to the table and ate my dinner as usual. My eyes would close. I felt like laughing and joking. I knew then what had happened. I knew that Brother Sheffey had prayed for me somewhere. On Monday mother came back to see me. She said, 'Oh! Mary, what has happened to you? You are so much better.' I told her I knew that Brother Sheffey had prayed for me, but I didn't know where. Then she told me about sending the note to Brother Sheffey on Saturday before. I am sixty-seven years old and I have always believed in prayer. I am the daughter of Mr. and Mrs. E. A. Davis and Brother Sheffey visited in our home many times."

Writing on "Preachers and Religion of the Mountains Fifty Years Ago" the Rev. William Henry Book of Orlando, Florida, published the following article in the New Castle (Va.) Record. The date of the publication of the article is not known. It came into our possession through a friend living at Bastian, Va. It follows:

"One of the most unique and original preachers of the past century was Robert Sayers Sheffey.... He was a true type of the John Wesley Methodists. He was in every sense of the word, a circuit rider. He was in many ways, a free lance, and no set of bishops could boss him. He would leave his home unannounced and be gone for weeks. Out into the mountain gorges and into the little villages he went with his type of religion. He was more of an exhorter than he was a preacher. He had a passion for souls. He labored diligently resting upon the promises of God for his support. He knew what it was to sacrifice the comforts of life and to give himself for others. He was a welcome guest in the homes of Christian people; but distillers and gamblers were afraid of him. I have heard of the way he would go to a man's still and get down on his knees and pray for it to be destroyed, and soon after that earnest prayer, a storm or a fire would make havoc of it. He made it his business to pray in front of stills, and he was a holy terror in the presence of the liquor dealer. He had the reputation of being a man of earnest prayer and one who received answers to his prayers.

"When I was pastor in Pulaski, I visited a family that had moved from Bland county to Pulaski. They brought the family cow with them and she had departed from the new home and had been gone a number of days. The members of that family were greatly disturbed and feared the cow was gone for good. The evening before my visit, Brother Sheffey had called and they told him of their grief. He got down on his knees and prayed earnestly that the cow might return, and then said, 'She will come home.' They said, 'Sure enough, that evening after his prayer, the old cow came walking in.'

"He was fond of honey and, he invariably, after eating to his fill of honey and the honey-comb, would shout and sing. He believed in shouting. He thought it was evidence of the presence of the Holy Ghost when he felt good. He was also very fond of chicken and dumplings. I have heard this story: One day he stopped in the home of a friend. The lady had cooked a fat hen for dinner. Many good things were on the table, but it was the hen that got his attention. When the sister asked him to offer grace, he said: 'Lord, we thank Thee for this good woman; we thank Thee for this good dinner, and we thank Thee for this good chicken; but it would have been better had it had dumplings in it. Amen.'

"He was the evangelist and the pastor of the mountain people in Giles, Bland, Pulaski, Tazewell, Smyth and Mercer counties. He traveled thousands of miles through all kinds of weather. He lived in the log huts with the poor. He prayed in their homes and read to them the Scriptures. The people believed in his sincerity. His life was an open book and they recognized it as being an epistle of Christ. He believed in the Bible from 'kiver to kiver.' He was not bothered with destructive criticism. He lived in a day when the people heard little of "higher criticism' or 'destructive criticism.' It was then called 'Thos. Paine's Doctrine' or 'Ingersollism.' It was a straight-forward infidelity. Now it is known as 'Unitarianism' or 'Culture.' Just the same old child of the devil in a dress of another color. The life and influence of Robert Sheffey was worth more to a community than all the 'Tom' Paines and Robert Ingersolls that have lived in two generations. Methodist success in Southwest Virginia has been largely due to the life and teachings of Robert Sheffey. He was the John the Baptist of this denomination in this section of the state. The people are proud to entertain visitors today by relating the experiences of this good man. Few song books were in the homes of the people. When they gathered for worship in an humble school house on a mountain side or down in the valley, 'at early candle lighting,' the minister held the song book in his hand and lined the hymn for the people to sing. He generally led the singing. That was before we had organs or pianos. Long before the pipe organ. No high-sounding music in that day with the good old time mountain people, but they sang from the heart, and they did it lustily, too. The people had not begun to debate the question of instrumental music. The fiddle, now called the violin, was believed to be an instrument of the devil, and had anyone brought an instrument into the house of God he would have been ex-communicated in short order. Old-fashioned people, and it did stir the the souls of men and women.

"Long shall live the memory of Robert Sheffey in the counties of Southwest Virginia."

An interesting visit with Esq. H. B. Kitts, of Bluefield, W. Va., brought to his recollection an incident that had to do with his marriage in Mercer county, W. Va., more than sixty-five years ago. At the Alvis camp ground, situated upon the present site of the Virginian railway shops, in Princeton, it came to the ears of Brother Sheffey that Mr. Kitts and Miss Minnie Kahle, sister of the late Rev. E. F. Kahle, were to be married at a certain time in the future. He announced to the prospective groom that he would be on hand for the wedding. The marriage took place in the year 1881, at New Hope, near Princeton. About seventy-five guests were present. And, according to promise, so was Brother Sheffey. In the evening a large number of young people in the community arranged to serenade the couple. As they approached the house they met Brother Sheffey and he urged them to return to their homes and "let them good people alone." And not content with this admonition, he proceeded to pray about the matter. In a very brief period of time the group had dispersed and the happy young couple were left to enjoy the evening without the interruption of the serenaders.

Esq. Kitts was the son of Peter Kitts of Bland courthouse. He knew much about the wanderings of the itinerant preachers. He recalled how a certain presiding elder, when he had come to the Radford district, decided that he would abandon the camp meetings at the Wabash camp ground in Giles county. This provoked Brother Sheffey, who was a firm believer in these meetings. At a service held near Wabash he prayed about this as he did about everything else. In his prayer he asked the Lord to bless our presiding elder in his big ways and his little ways. And he added, "In our sight he is but small potatoes and few in a hill."

Mrs. Ed Deaton, of Bluefield, Virginia, is a niece of Brother Sheffey, a sister of the late Daily Stafford, of Trigg, Va. She remembers her illustrious uncle with tenderest affection. It was she who gave us a most interesting explanation of Brother Sheffey's excessive fondness for sweets of every description. Before he was converted he liked the taste of whiskey very much. He prayed that "the Lord might take the whiskey taste away and give him a taste for sweet things." He always said that the Lord heard and answered this prayer in a very definite way.

Mrs. Deaton also told us about Mrs. Elbert Johnson, at Trigg, Va., who had eight sons and four daughters. The sons "took to railroading." The mother was uneasy and feared that some of her boys might be killed in a railroad accident. One day she mentioned the uneasiness that constantly dwelt with her, and asked Brother Sheffey to pray that her sons might be saved from such an accident. One day he came by the Johnson home and told the mother that she need not have any further worry; that he had "Talked with the Lord" and that He had promised him that they would be saved from such an untimely end. His prayers were answered. The sons were spared.

Mrs. Will J. Crockett who lives in Bluefield, Virginia was converted in a revival meeting held on Clear Fork in Tazewell county, Va., where Brother Sheffey was assisting in a revival. She was only twelve years of age. While at the altar this good man of God came to her and tenderly prayed that this little girl might be saved from her sins. She recalls how God's Spirit bore witness with her own spirit that she had been saved and there was great joy in her heart. The years passed by and the life of this lady was to be touched again by that old saint of God, but in another way. She was 24 years of age, married, and the mother of a little girl about two months old. Both of them were desperately ill and their lives were hanging in balance. A messenger had been hurriedly despatched for Dr. J. R. Hicks at Shawver's Mill. On the way he met Brother Sheffey and told him about the illness of the mother and daughter. He prayed for their recovery and after that the family were at ease in their minds. Who will dare say that God who hears the prayers of the righteous man did not work through the physician to aid him in his ministrations which made possible their recovery? Mrs. Crockett also told us how the prayers of Brother Sheffey were answered in the destruction of a distillery near Rocky Gap, in Bland county. The plant was located about the foot of a steep hill. There were no trees about it, but in Brother Sheffey's prayer he asked God to send a tree down across the plant and wreck it. Many people said that here was one prayer of Sheffey's that would not be answered. Far up on the hill stood an old tree. The storm came and one who saw it said the tree zig-zagged down the hillside and finally plunged into the still tearing it to pieces. In his prayer he had also asked God to convert the place into a sheep pen and the farm was afterwards rented by Wm. E. Neel, an uncle of Mrs. Crockett. Assisting him was a man who heard Brother Sheffey's prayer and as they worked he recalled that prayer.

Rev. George W. Fox, retired pastor at North Tazewell, member of Holston conference, sends us part of a prayer said to have been used quite often by Brother Sheffey. He said that he asked Rev. J. S. W. Neal about whether or not he had ever heard Brother Sheffey make use of these words in his prayer and he said, "I don't remember to have ever heard him say it, but it is so much like many things that I have heard him say that I am sure that he did say it." He also adds: "Brother Neal knew Sheffey as well as anyone could know a man, and loved him as he could love, and appreciated him for what he was—a man of God." Here is the quotation with which he would sometimes conclude his prayer: "Now, Lord, when I have done all on earth that I can do, let me die, and take me home to heaven. There let me dive down into the River of Life, and come up about fifty yards from where I went in; then make a lake of tree molasses, and a fritter cake tree to grow right up in the middle of it; send an angel up to shake the fritters down, give me a golden fork, let me dip in, and live forever."

The late Leroy Landrum, local preacher and member of Trinity church, Bluefield, W. Va., says that he attended the dedication of a church near Newbern, in Pulaski county, Va., more than a half century ago. The pastor announced that there was an outstanding indebtedness against the church and that this sum must be paid before the dedication services were concluded. Brother Sheffey happened to be present. He announced that he would give five dollars but that he did not have a dime in his pocket. He knelt on his sheep-skin near the altar and asked the Lord to make it possible for him to get the amount he had offered. At the conclusion of his prayer a gentleman in the rear of the building held up his hand and said, "Here is five dollars for Brother Sheffey."

Here are two incidents given by Mrs. Lester S. Parsons, of Norfolk, Va., a daughter of the late Rev. J. A. H. Shuler of the Methodist church, a sister of Dr. Ellis W. Shuler, connected with the Southern Methodist University at Dallas, Texas, and a first cousin of "Bob" Shuler, well known member of the California conference. Once at a camp meeting Brother Sheffey was praying in the tent of Rev. James Fisher about a man whom he wanted saved. He didn't know his name and he sought to describe him to God by telling him about his hat and his coat and the way he had his hair combed. He said, "And Dear Heavenly Father, bless the brother over in the corner who is unknown to thy servant, but from the shape of his pants and the cut of his coat I think he is from Grayson county."

Here is another incident given by Mrs. Parsons who was present and witnessed what happened. "One scene is indelibly stamped upon my memory. We were at a church near Mechanicsburg and Brother Sheffey was to preach. He was so long in arriving that a young preacher talked at length and when Brother Sheffey did arrive he preached for an hour, (and no preacher in those days was worth his salt who couldn't hold forth for an hour). We had all been invited over to the Shannon home for dinner. Brother Sheffey was late in arriving.... We had had a long dry spell that year and the blades of the corn were curled and browning. We needed rain. "Uncle Bob" was fed most regally by the women folk. Honey flavored with coffee, special piece of pie, extra large dish of home-made ice cream. I know because I was one of the children who stood in the dining room door and watched him eat. Then he took another cup of the same brew and went down in the great lawn and stooped in under a huge Deodora Cedar by the gate. This time he knelt on the pine needles and prayed something like this: 'O Good God, can't you see we need rain. You said if I asked you'd give it to me. Dear Father, I'm asking you now for rain. Thank you, Lord.' When he went under the tree there were no clouds in the sky but before three o'clock they gathered quickly and by five they poured forth their healing upon the thirsty earth and we all marvelled at the gift of prayer." Mrs. Parsons adds: "He has a cave named for him as well as hundreds of men and women. I have been in the cave."

Chapter VIII

Other Sheffey Stories

Another very interesting story which reveals the generosity of the heart and soul of this old country preacher and explains why he was universally beloved was first told us by George S. Strader, Bluefield, West Virginia, business man. Mr. Strader was a youth of tender years in the Staffordsville, Giles county, community, when Brother Sheffey was most active in his missionary work and remembers him quite well. The facts in the story came to us from William C. Thomas, a prominent attorney of Wytheville, Va.

One hot summer day Brother Sheffey was riding horseback from Wytheville to Bland courthouse, on the Raleigh and Grayson turn-pike, and just as he reached the top of Big Walker's mountain he met a covered wagon, heavily loaded, bound for North Carolina. One of the horses of this team had become over-heated and dropped dead about the top of the mountain. Of course, the driver was very much worried about how he could continue on to his destination. Brother Sheffey rode up and said: "Stranger, I see you are in distress; unhitch your dead horse and drag him aside and you can hitch mine up in its place." The driver said, "How will I return him to you?" Brother Sheffey said, "You won't have to return him; I am making you a present of this horse, and the good Lord will soon provide me with another horse." The driver thanked Brother Sheffey very profusely and proceeded on his journey. The preacher walked into Bland courthouse carrying his saddle and bridle, and Harman Newberry and Thomas Findlay, two well-to-do farmers, who were sitting on a store porch asked Brother Sheffey why he was walking. He told them he had just befriended a brother and gave them his story. These gentlemen told Brother Sheffey that a drove of unbroken western horses had just arrived at the Bland courthouse and were to be auctioned off that afternoon and that they would buy the best horse in the drove and make him a present of it. The best looking horse in the drove was lassoed and given to Brother Sheffey by these two gentlemen. They told Brother Sheffey that they would get some man to break the horse for him, as it had never been ridden before. Brother Sheffey said, "No, that will be unnecessary; just have the horse led up to me." This was done and Brother Sheffey put his hand on the shoulder of the animal and made a short prayer, and told them to put the saddle and bridle on the horse, and he got on him and rode down towards Giles county without the least trouble. Mr. Thomas says the story was related to him by an eye-witness to the occurrence.

Mr. Thomas recalls a certain visit Brother Sheffey made to the home of his grandfather, William G. Crockett, Crockett's Cove, Wythe county, Va., some sixty odd years ago when he was a child. Speaking of these periodical visits he says: "On one of these visits of Brother Sheffey to my grandfather's, I was visiting there. I was subject to the croup, when I was a small boy and on this occasion, I woke in the night with a severe attack of this disease, and my grandparents were very much alarmed about my condition and aroused Brother Sheffey and had him to pray for my recovery, which he was glad to do. His prayer on this occasion was certainly answered for I have lived for more than a half century since that prayer was uttered."

Quoting Mr. Thomas further: "A short time before Brother Sheffey's death he was holding a meeting at Siloam church in Wythe county and he heard in advance that two men were contemplating the erection of a bar-room just across the road from that church. These prospective bar-keepers thought that Brother Sheffey would refer to their undertaking at his first service, so they attended that service. Brother Sheffey made a very fervent prayer and told the Lord that two men were thinking of erecting a bar-room within the shadow of the church and he asked the Lord to change the minds of these wicked men. He also asked the Lord if He would not change their minds to strike them down dead and remove them from the face of the earth. After the service was over these men told several people that they would make anybody a present of the bar-room lot, as they were afraid of Brother Sheffey's prayers being answered. This bar was never erected at the proposed location.

The next instance happened at Bland courthouse. Brother Sheffey went to a lawyer's office in that village. The office was located in one end of the building with a chimney in the middle. Brother Sheffey asked the lawyer if that was a bar-room, in the other end of the building, and he told him it was. Brother Sheffey knelt down in the lawyer's office and prayed to the Lord that the chimney would fall on the end of the house in which the bar-room was located. The lawyer stated that a few weeks after this, he was sitting in his office and he heard the plaster begin to fall, and that the chimney fell over and caved in the roof to the room in which the saloon was located.

A year before Brother Sheffey's death he sold his riding horse to a man in Grayson county, Virginia, for $200 cash. About a month after the sale Brother Sheffey visited the purchaser of the horse and told him that he had talked with the Lord and that the Lord had told him that he received $25 too much for the horse. He refunded the $25 to the purchaser of the animal which was very reluctantly received.

In offering these stories, Mr. Thomas said: "My uncle, William Chaffin Crockett, who died in 1921, preached Brother Sheffey's funeral. I have often heard my uncle say that Brother Sheffey had some unusual power, and he seemed to get closer to the Lord than any other person that he knew."

W. A. Saferight, of Wytheville, says that he attended a revival meeting held by Brother Sheffey in Bland county many years ago where a large number of persons were converted. There was a young man in the neighborhood who had been attending the services. He was quite rough and notwithstanding the persistent efforts of the workers to get him to the altar he refused to move. Brother Sheffey called to him and said that the Lord was inviting him to respond to the invitations of the preacher and that if he continued to refuse some misfortune would befall him before the next night. This did not move him. He worked at a sawmill nearby and sure enough he suffered the misfortune to get his arm caught in a belt and it had to be amputated. Mr. Saferight said he talked with this man many times after his accident. For many years he lived at Wytheville but is now dead. Mr. Saferight also tells about a man by the name of Williams who was desperately ill, in fact, he was at the point of death. He says that "we got Sheffey and asked him to go up and pray for him, which he did, and after he got up he said he would be all right." He recovered. He declares that the power that Sheffey had in prayer he had never seen in any other man, and he added, that when he began to shout there was "an extra light from his head."

Mrs. T. M. Cassell, of Ceres, Bland county, Va., says that she remembers Brother Sheffey quite well; that he was a frequent visitor in the home of her father, Rev. L. M. Bruce, Methodist minister, now dead. She said that her father used to preach at Zion, in Bland county, on the second Sunday in each month. He passed two still-houses on his way to his appointments. These places were a source of trouble in the neighborhood and she recalls that she had to pass them when a little girl going to and from school. More than once she came very near being run down by drunken riders on horseback. She grew to be very nervous because of her experiences. Her father tried through prayer and other means to rid the community of these vicious influences, but his efforts failed. He wrote Brother Sheffey and asked him to talk to the Lord about these places and he answered that he would. In a short time he notified the Rev. Bruce that he had received an answer to his prayer and that in a very short time one of them would be a hog sty and the other a sheep pen. And "it came around in that very way." Mrs. Cassell says that she has a cousin who declares that if Brother Sheffey had been alive at the time Hitler was wrecking the world that there would soon "be no Hitler"—that's how much faith my cousin has in Sheffey, says Mrs. Cassell.

Mrs. Nannie Jackson Wassom, of Wytheville, gives us the following interesting letter regarding Brother Sheffey. Brief paragraphs have been omitted but the major part of the letter is offered giving a brief picture of Sheffey: "I am the oldest daughter of Rev. R. F. Jackson, who was a member of Holston conference for many years. Before my father finally decided to preach he had a very serious illness—was ill for several months at the home of my grandfather, James Early, who lived on Cripple Creek, near Ivanhoe, Va.

"Across the creek and up among the hills from the Early home was the Sheffey home—I've heard my grandmother tell of how he visited father during his illness, praying for him and assuring the family his prayers would be answered and he would be restored to health.

"People in that section were firm believers in Mr. Sheffey's prayers and it is told that the liquor people had an especial fear of him, for when he prayed for stills to be destroyed they were.

"My first and only acquaintance with him was about 1900. Father was on the Bane circuit in Giles county, near the Old Wabash Camp Ground. One Sunday morning at Lebanon church, the service had begun and I was playing the organ possibly for the opening song when a rather small, peculiar looking grey-haired (his hair was long and he often combed it when talking) man, carrying a small sheep-skin, walked down the aisle and seated himself in the amen corner. Something told me this was Robert Sayers Sheffey of whom I had heard so much. Father called on him to pray and as I remember his prayer it was earnest but rather disconnected and very lengthy. When he apparently was ready to conclude, he convulsed the younger members of the congregation by saying, 'And now one more word, dear Lord. Bless that pretty little girl that tries to sing and play the organ!'

"For several days he was in the neighborhood and spent part of the time in our home. On the bureau in his room he had carried from the table and placed there—honey, cakes, sweets of various kinds. At dinner one day when mother started to cut a damson pie topped with whipped cream he said, 'Now, sister be sure to use a clean knife to cut that pie.' He had a habit of writing his name and making little drawings around on the walls and buildings. He rode a bay horse and would often dismount to pray by the roadside.

"I think it was in 1902 that father heard of him being

sick at the home of a relative at White Gate or near there and he drove from Bane, (a day's trip), to see him. Then when he died and was buried at Wesley's Chapel, in Giles county, he conducted the funeral.

"My impression of him was that though very eccentric, he was a godly man. A man who really believed in prayer and convinced others of its power and he made a vital and lasting contribution to the religious history of that section."

The late James H. Summers, Bluefield, Va., tells us of a prayer that Brother Sheffey prayed during a visit into the Bluestone area adjacent to what is now known as the Springville community. A distillery was being operated near this place and its evil influence was being felt upon many lives and in many homes. The prayer ran something like this: "Lord, there is an old still being run in this neighborhood. Too many people are drinking liquor. I want you to burn it down. Don't let anybody get hurt. Put out the fire before it has burned completely down. Take the mud sills and let some man make a carpenter shop out of them where useful things can be made for the homes and farms. Let the foundation rocks be turned into the cornerstones of a church." Some time later Green Ferguson built a carpenter's shop out of those very sills and the rocks were turned into a foundation for the Springville church. Some of the Ferguson furniture for many years adorned the Summers home.

Brother Sheffey was a frequent visitor in the home of Mr. and Mrs. W. N. Mustard, near Bland courthouse. Upon one occasion Mrs. Mustard had knitted a pair of socks for the preacher and when he came that way she presented him with them. He had scarcely gotten out of sight of the Mustard home until he met with Giles Thomas, a laborer on the Mustard farm. Thomas had no socks. It was a bitter cold day. Brother Sheffey decided that Thomas needed the socks more than he did so he gave them over to the man who put them on and went up to the Mustard home to work. Mrs. Mustard saw them and asked him where he got them. He replied that Brother Sheffey had given them to him.

A visit with Mrs. Sarah Catherine Wheeler, 93 year old

grandmother of Mrs. Henderson Lambert, of Narrows, brought forth an odd story which occurred in the Staffordsville community where Mrs. Wheeler was reared. A man had lost a cow. She had been gone for sometime. One day Brother Sheffey came by while the search for the cow was still going on. Someone told him about the cow's disappearance. He remarked that he would pray about the cow and ask the Lord to see that she returned home. In a short time the cow appeared at her accustomed place when milking time had arrived.

Praying was as natural for Brother Sheffey as breathing. He always resorted to prayer as regularly as he would do anything else. Mrs. Helen Coeburn, of Narrows, said that the preacher came to Narrows one day and was at some church service. He had failed to put a handkerchief in his pocket when he started to church so he asked Mrs. Josie Johnson, a sister of Mrs. Coeburn, to give him a handkerchief. She did so and that evening in the service he prayed for "that woman who gave him a handkerchief." Mrs. Josie Johnson was the mother of Thomas J. Johnson, assistant cashier of the First National Bank of Narrows.

J. Bowman Stafford, of Staffordsville, Virginia, a son of Dr. Daniel Hoge Stafford, brother of Mrs. Robert Sayers Sheffey, who spent the last seven nights with Mrs. Sheffey before her death, gave us this interesting story which he said could be verified by George Carr, an aged citizen of the Staffordsville community, who was present at the time of the incident recorded. A group of men were engaged in logging near White Gate, Va. One of their horses had fallen into a sink-hole and mired up until it looked like it would be impossible to extricate the animal. Brother Sheffey appeared about this time and discovered the predicament of the horse. He told the men to leave the animal alone until he came back. He rode off down the hillside to the creek and got down and prayed for a time and then he took the halter, (he always had a halter under his bridle), off his own horse, put the bridle back on, tied the horse to a limb, and walked back up to the men who were standing around the helpless animal. He walked over and placed his own halter on the horse and said, "Now, come on." The horse quietly walked out of the miry hole into which it had fallen. All this he did quietly and without a moment's hesitation. He seemed to know that that horse was going to do exactly what it did do.

Mr. Stafford also recited a story told to him by the Rev. John D. Dame, honored member of the Holston conference from 1855 to 1933. On one of the charges served by Brother Dame during his ministry he lived in a house that had formerly been used as a still-house. It had been converted into a Methodist parsonage. The barn where the preacher kept his horse had formerly been a mill house where the grain had been ground for the distillery. At the time the distillery was in operation Brother Sheffey appeared in the community and held a meeting. He prayed that the still-house might be converted into a home for a Methodist preacher and the mill house into a barn for the preacher's horse. The very things for which he prayed came to pass in the providence of God.

Speaking of the death of Mrs. Sheffey, Mr. Stafford said that at the instruction of his father, Dr. Stafford, brother of Mrs. Sheffey and her physician, he cared for her much of the time during her last illness. Her death was occasioned by remittent attacks of fever. The night she died, so he says, Brother Sheffey sang the song that was perhaps his greatest favorite. It was the song he sang so often, "Twilight is stealing over the lea." And at her funeral, at his own request, he was permitted to say a few words which were quite affecting and moved the entire congregation to tears.

Mrs. Andrew Suiter, who once lived at Nemours, W. Va., tells a story very much like that of Rev. Dame. On a farm in Bland county there was a distillery being operated by a certain man. The whiskey was injuring the community morale and causing much trouble generally because of its widespread influence. Brother Sheffey came into the community and held a meeting. He prayed that the distillery might be converted into a sheep house, a cattle house, or a dwelling house. In the course of time it was used for all three of these purposes.

On another farm in Bland county, about four miles above Rocky Gap, a distillery was being operated, according to Mrs. Suiter, and the old preacher prayed for its destruction and a storm demolished the entire plant. And in the Clear Fork section of Bland county, near what is called the Mt. Calvary church, (then a school house), a man by the name of Underwood was running a distillery. A meeting was in progress at the school house and Brother Sheffey prayed that the Lord might destroy the plant. His prayer ran something like this: "O Lord, if there is no other way to get this thing stopped send some affliction on the man who is operating the place." Mrs. Suiter says that about three months later a cancer came on the face of the man and he ceased his accursed business.

It was Mrs. Suiter who showed us the sheepskin, in the Davidson home, formerly used by Brother Sheffey and made mention of in another place in these writings. That sheepskin was given to Rev. Peter Rayburn Suiter, local preacher in the Methodist church for many years in Bland county and an associate of the itinerant preacher. Brother Sheffey gave the skin to Mr. Suiter and it in turn has been handed down to the children of Joe Davidson, direct descendants of Suiter. Another of these skins became the property of a Mrs. Yost, near Graton church, in Tazewell county. Mrs. Suiter also prizes a piece of a door facing taken from an old house in which Rev. J. S. W. Neel and family lived at Cove Creek. On this piece of timber Brother Sheffey had drawn a number of pictures during one of his periodical visits to the Neel home.

Speaking of prayer, Mrs. Suiter recalled that she heard Brother Sheffey say upon one occasion that he would not ask the Lord for unreasonable things. He said to pray for eleven wagons loaded with sugar would be unreasonable, and, of course, the Lord would not hear a prayer like that. But, he declared, the Lord would answer any reasonable prayer for one of his children. And the old preacher believed every word of that statement.

Mrs. Martin Luther ("Ed") Carter, residing at Flat Top Yards, Virginia, said that she remembered a visit of Brother Sheffey to the neighborhood of Falls Mills in her girlhood days. There was a meeting going on at the church and near the church was a saloon operated by a Capt. Cooper. Mrs. Carter, (then a Miss Mullins) said that Brother Sheffey prayed for the destruction of the saloon and in a very short time thereafter the place was burned to the ground.

Brother Sheffey was visiting at the home of some friends up Wolf Creek, above Narrows, and he walked up into the woods to pray. In that home was a boy named Rafe Alvis. Young Alvis wondered where the old preacher was going. He decided that he would find out. He had a dog that was quite adept at the art of trailing and so he sent the dog after Brother Sheffey. Finally he located the preacher who was engaged in prayer. The dog became so fierce in his approach that Brother Sheffey had to call for help. Soon the boy appeared and "called off" his dog. The preacher walked up to young Alvis, stroked him on the head and said, "God bless you, sonny; you are the boy that sicked the dog on me."

Matthew Ellis Bailey related the following incident to Rev. John B. Staley, at the time the pastor of the Methodist church at Montcalm. About the year 1883 Mr. Bailey lived not far from the Clark's Gap community in Mercer county, W. Va., and Brother Sheffey following out his preaching tours would stop at the Bailey home. In that community the preacher had announced that he would start a revival at a school house on a certain date. The time had arrived and in company with Mr. Bailey they repaired to the appointed place, but there was not a single soul in sight. No one appeared for the service. As the two were returning to the Bailey home the old preacher gave out a sad prophecy. Said he, "A great calamity will come to this community, and you will see it." Mr. Bailey tells how in a few months a terrible epidemic of small-pox struck that community and took a great majority of the people away. Whole families were taken, and often days would elapse before many of them were found.

Following out this story, the author having preached near the Clark's Gap community, a letter was addressed to a member of his former congregation at Beartown, on the Crumpler charge, and a reply was received on August 7, 1940, which tells in vivid style of the facts concerning this scourge of small-pox to that neighborhood. In fact, the man who wrote the letter says, "I was one among those stricken by the calamity." Today he bears striking evidence of the seriousness of this plague. That letter comes from C. D. Blankenship, member of the Prosperity Methodist church on the Crumpler charge in the Bluefield district.

Here are some excerpts from the Blankenship letter: "Ellis Bailey and I grew up together. I knew him and I knew Brother Sheffey. I've heard him preach several times. He sure told Ellis there would be a great calamity sent on the people.

"My uncle, Wade Blankenship, was the first one to take the small-pox and died before the people knew what it was. Many people turned out to attend the burial. Forty-eight persons took the disease and died at the same time I was down.... My dad was keeping store at that time. He and uncle Wade went to Charleston, W. Va., to lay in a lot of goods, and coming back between Charleston and Hinton the conductor stopped the train and put off a negro with the small-pox. Uncle Wade contracted it here and that is how it got started.

"When my uncle died they sent to Pocahontas and got old Dr. Hess and he pronounced it chicken pox. The people kept on dying so fast and they decided to send to Hinton, W. Va., to get a doctor. They got one by the name of Gooch. He came and pronounced it small-pox and immediately he set about to vaccinate the people.... I had a brother that was so bad that they had his coffin made. He did not die, and when he got up to going around he got in the coffin and said it was too short for him.... There was one family of five—the whole five lay dead at one time, and the nurse old Captain Grigsby wanted to set the house on fire and burn them up."

Rev. E. C. Williams, local preacher in the Methodist church for many years and now residing at Newbern, Va., gave a story about a still-house in the Newbern community known as the Alexander distillery. It was located near the Alexander mill. Brother Sheffey was holding a meeting in that neighborhood more than a half century ago. He prayed that God would convert the distillery into a meeting-house. Thirty years later this place became a Christian church and the first preacher was Rev. J. A. Shelburne of the Christian denomination.

Brother Sheffey once said that the Lord had fed him on the fat of the land. Everywhere he went, he said the people fixed him something good to eat.

Speaking of medicines one day he said, "Nice, clean salt is the best medicine in the world."

The old preacher, about middle life, began to wear a heavy beard. He was telling a friend on one occasion how it was that he never shaved any more. He said he was riding along one day and a severe hail storm struck him full in the face and cut his cheeks in a number of places. He declared that the Lord told him that a beard would protect his face and that he had worn one ever since.

Brother Sheffey did not have time to dwell on the common-place things of this world. Rather his mind, his soul, his whole thought dwelt upon God and Christ and the things that pertained to the Christian religion. He wouldn't have known anything about theology had he come face to face with it, but he had religion, and he knew all about the fundamentals of theology. For all true theology must find its basic facts in God. Here he stopped. He was satisfied with God—with God he had everything that heaven and earth could offer him.

One day he began to write in a book what at first glance appeared to be sermon notes on God. But they were not, for I am quite sure that he never used a sermon note in all his preaching. Here are some of his thoughts:

"What is more beautiful than the rose? God.

"What is fairer than the lily? God.

"What is there in all the universe of God that is the most beautiful? God.

"What would you love to see in heaven? God, our Great King.

"What is the Light of Heaven? God.

"The night and day are both alike to God. He can see day and night. God never sleeps. God is happy day and night. Why? Because His thoughts, actions and words are all right. Thou God seest us both day and night. How sweet, how grand, how glorious, how delightful, and how pleasant is our sweet Lord to His children. Why? Because God is love; God is good; God is a spirit; God is merciful; God is just; God is full of good qualities, and not any bad qualities. God's words, thoughts, and actions have always been right and shall always be right. Nothing superior to God; His power, mercy, love, and presence, and wisdom, are great and are unbounded. Let us be in love with Him always and trust in Him and work for Him and He will compensate us here and hereafter in sweet heaven."

And then the old warrior's thoughts began to turn toward the Holy City for he writes: "No night in Heaven. There are twelve manner of fruits in glory and they are superfine. Twelve foundations to the walls of the Golden City. Pure gold is the composition of the streets of the city. Never get sick in glory or in the Golden City. I want to get there, don't you?"

On another page he has written what were like proverbs to him. They are words of truth. They sound like some of the Proverbs we read in the Book. But he had his own quaint way of saying things, and we understand at once that he was no stranger to God's word. Here are his sayings: "The greatest wisdom of speech is to know when and where and what to speak. The next to it is silence. Never talk too much. In the multitude of words there wanteth not sin. He that keepeth his tongue in his mouth keepeth his soul from trouble. Religion is an innocent, pleasant and glorious enjoyment. Religion affords us wisdom. May we learn how to be wise in the things of God."

Chapter IX

Sheffey's Travels

There is but little doubt that Sheffey traveled many thousands of miles across the hill country of Southwestern Virginia and the tip of Southern West Virginia in his endeavors to extend the borders of the Kingdom of God. He did not seek out the well-beaten paths that ran across this section. Rather he went out "into the highways and hedges" to tell men and women of the miraculous power of the Christian gospel to redeem from sin. On the mountain tops, down in the hollows, across the gorges, over the creeks and rivers, out into the forests, wherever man found a place to build a cabin or rear a more pretentious home, to these the old circuit-rider found his way. And the memories of those visits linger with all who remember his face as well as those who have listened as children to the stories told of the visits and the happenings of other days when "Uncle Bob" Sheffey passed that way.

About once a year, usually in the fall and winter months, the people of almost every community came together in the old-fashioned revival services. These events were of more than passing interest to the people, and the whole countryside, almost without exception, turned out to them. These were times of refreshing, the tide-gates of joy were opened in the souls of Christian people, religious fervor was manifest in almost every center of the community and in most of the homes. People of those days believed in God; they didn't have much time to trifle with the little petty schemes that confound the minds of men today; modern-day amusements were unheard of; where God was in the life, He was the very center of that life.

Nothing gave Brother Sheffey more joy than to go into a community and conduct a revival. And at the revival season he was continuously engaged in this kind of work. Or if he happened in to a community where a revival was already in progress he joined his efforts with that of the preacher-in-charge to the end that there might be a great meeting. And he would labor just as earnestly in one meeting as another. Many are the souls that shall stand redeemed before God through the efforts of Robert Sayers Sheffey.

Sheffey was in the Dublin neighborhood, near Radford, where a meeting was being conducted by Rev. Charles W. Kelly. He spent the time at the home of James Trollinger, an estimable member of the church. During the meeting someone suggested, in the Trollinger home, that Brother Sheffey sing and pray over the telephone so that the members of the party line might listen in and hear him. He accepted the suggestion. The results were amazing to him. He wrote a letter back to some of his friends in which he says, "I prayed and sung near a telephone at Mr. Trollinger's, and it would sing and pray for us and utter the words sung and prayed. It is remarkable."

It is very doubtful whether Brother Sheffey ever forgot a friend or a kindness rendered him. He enjoyed writing to his friends, and would begin many of his letters by mentioning the names of those whom he remembered most in the community where the letter happened to be sent. I have a letter before me just now written from Lynchburg in 1897. It begins: "Dear ones, and all; Dr. Blackburn and family, and Brothers Floyd Vest and Calvin Best, and all that are near and dear to me in that part of the world, and especially Brother Aurelius Vest and his dear companion, and Sister Julia Bogle and all of the dear family there, and all of John Stinson's family, and Elizabeth Bussy, and especially Catherine Stafford and Susan Sexton and all her relations, Brother Warner and dear sweet family, and all enquiring friends." This letter was addressed to "Brother Aurelius Vest and others, White Gate, Giles county, Virginia," with appended foot-note: "P. M. Do your best for me. R. S. S."

In one of his letters written from Clearfork, Va., on September 25, 1900, he says that he is at the home of Dr. J. J. Bishop on his way to certain points in Bland and Giles counties, near the Bishop's chapel church. He writes: "I have been laboring on Wolf Creek and Clearfork in different ways—visiting, and traveling, and talking, reading, and preaching, and exhorting backwards and forwards since I started. This bright and beautiful day I got gloriously happy doing as I said since I came here, going without supper and eating what was necessary this morning, and that is a little juice from the bee combs."

This same journey carried him over into Tazewell county, to the Witten's Mill community. In the letter he says "I was at a noble meeting at May's Chapel church, (church named for a daughter of Gratton Mustard who subscribed perhaps $500 toward erecting the church). Good subscription certainly, if he did it to God's glory. I say glory to God for all that was paid by any." These words he appears to have added as an afterthought: "The wealth of the sinner is laid up for the just; the just shall live by faith." (Note—Miss May Mustard, for whom the church was named is now Mrs. H. S. Bowen, of Tazewell, Va. The writer was her pastor in 1938-39.)

In the same letter he writes: "I was at another meeting almost like a camp meeting in numbers. Good speaking, no converts, but good diet on the ground, good shade trees, good water. I was very much pleased with the churches —one Methodist and one Christian Baptist, at Falls Mills. I attended another meeting at Mt. Calvary church and we had a pleasant time, good sweet religion and good diet. Some breaking the Sabbath selling some things that ought to have been given away. 'The love of money is the root of all evil,' but I got some etc., and drank some and eat some to the glory of God."

Sheffey made occasional visits to the home of his son, Eddy, at Lynchburg. Edward Sheffey loved his father with all his heart and during his visits to the city he always tried to entertain him with the greatest consideration and affection. But the ways of the city were not the ways of the man who had given his life to his people of the hills. Writing from Lynchburg he said: "The people here who know how to be polite, they are very much so indeed. Some of them eat their provisions with a fork, but dry white sugar runs through in between the prongs and can't navigate good. They have a way to catch flies on a sticky piece of paper, and I tried to get the dear things out and some would fly away and some would die and some stick, and I would pour water on them to relieve them but could not." He said that he enjoyed the "good provisions, good ice water, and ice cream called orange ice cream, and other good things," since he had arrived in Lynchburg.

He visited the "female college," while on this visit, and said, "It is a great large building certainly. One man, Dr. Smith, gave about $11,000 and one man, Brother Pettyjohn gave about $5,000. They are raised in my estimation and in the estimation of other people in consideration of their liberal disposition and qualities. Dr. Smith was the man who got the project started, or my sweet Lord, he and Brother Pettyjohn. I got hold of him (Dr. Smith) after Sabbath School and embraced him, or hugged him, in consideration of his great benevolence."

Sheffey in a brief diary makes mention of a certain quarterly meeting which was to be held on June 22, 1901. He writes: "May my sweet Lord see to it that both human beings and animals be cared for at the various places or plantations, and may all the preachers and laborers and church members of every denomination and the people be seen to and their need supplied."

Sheffey's diary reveals his tender affection for the horse which carried him through his many journeyings up and down, and over and across his circuit. He mentions his horse a number of times in the course of his diary and on one page he records: "Thanks to Charles Thomas Robert for carrying me and helping me so much during my life and his life over the hills and the mountains, and along the valleys, and across the streams, quicksands, and mud, and roads, rough, frozen and otherwise, bad weather, good weather, pleasant, or otherwise, to the various churches or houses and carrying me home and from home many a mile on this earth, and may God and I and the people be good and kind to him. Glory to God for him!"

When he would go to visit his son in Lynchburg he would usually ride across the mountain from Staffordsville to Dublin. Here he would take the train, but first there must be proper arrangements made for the care of his horse. At the age of 81 years he made one of his visits. In his writings we find these words: "May the sweet Lord help me and my animal in going to Lynchburg and returning from Lynchburg. Show me when to get on the cars or train, please Sir, and take care of my horse in my absence.

Show me how to get him cared for; show me how to get a minister's ticket if this is your sweet will. May I be privileged to spend the 4th of July, 1901, at Lynchburg, at 'Eddy's' home. Nearly 81 years ago I saw the light first and was born on July 4, 1820, at Ivanhoe, Wythe county, Va. May I live as long as my dear Lord wants me to live. Glory to God! Lord, you are so sweet, and good, and noble-hearted, kind, and affectionate, and my benefactor."

Brother Sheffey's horse knew his master's will and his voice. The old circuit-rider had him so well trained that he would walk up to the fence and allow him to get on his back while he stood perfectly still. He was a large bay horse weighing about 1600 pounds. Brother Sheffey was a rather small man, about five feet and six inches tall, and weighed approximately 155 pounds. So it became necessary for him to resort to some method by which he could mount his horse with ease in the more advanced years of his life. He had taught his horse how he could best mount him, and this the animal seemed to thoroughly understand. The horse was as calm as he could be while Sheffey was astride him, but if someone else attempted to ride him there was trouble. The horse didn't like it, and he didn't fail to show his dislike for the rider.

Numbers of people have told the writer how they had seen the circuit-rider dismount when he came to a steep grade, even though it may have been but a few hundred yards distant, and lead his horse up the incline to the top of the hill. He would also use great precaution in what he fed the animal and how he watered him. And when he stopped over-night, or for a meal, at some place he would give instructions as to how the horse must be cared for. He would even measure the length of the ears of corn to be fed to the horse on his arm. A certain number of ears—no more, no less,—those were his instructions. He had ridden over the country so much and so often that he had special places for watering his horse. Sometimes he would call for a bucket and go to the spring for water rather than to allow his horse to drink out of a branch. It is said that after the horse became old in years and could not eat very well that the old preacher would place sugar and salt on the corn trying to coax him to eat. Many are the stories that are told about Sheffey and his horse. We do not wonder at these stories, for they were companions in storm and sunshine, they loved each other. A slight to Sheffey's horse was a slight to Sheffey. He would see that his horse was taken care of even though he himself had to go hungry.

When the time had arrived to seek out some place to spend the night, Sheffey would seek a home where he could find those comforts which his heart and body craved. He enjoyed sleeping in a bed with a white counterpane over the covers. At the home of Aurelius Vest, where he spent his last days and where he was often a guest during his active ministry, the good house-wife saw to it that his bed was clean and white, and a perfectly white counterpane spread over the coverings.

He also liked to go places where he knew that the housewife was likely to have those things to eat that suited his appetite. The things he liked most were as he writes them in his diary: "God's tree molasses and tree sugar, and sweet white sugar and coffee, sweet honey and the honey comb, corn bread, mush and cream, hominy, chicken and dumplings."

The brief diary of Sheffey reveals many interesting sidelights on the character of the old preacher. Wherever he came into a meeting of any kind and an offering was being taken he would contribute to the cause even though he never had a cent of money on his person. He always knew that God would provide the amount and sometime during the year he would see that it was paid according to promise. Sometimes he would ask certain persons to pay the amount for him and he would repay them at a later date. He mentions a number of contributions that he made to "the benevolent causes" of the church—one to Brother Handy, one to Brother French, one to Brother Crockett. Also contributions he made to certain church enterprises across his circuit. When he found people in need he would make an effort to relieve their condition by making provision for them. One case: "I left word for the miller, Mr. Witten, to send one bushel of meal to John W_____ and family who live on Mr. Robert Harman's place." A number of obligations he had made for as little as five cents were recorded in his book and there were later notations to the effect that they had been paid. One interesting notation reads like this: "The amount I thought I subscribed at Mt. Calvary for benevolences, I paid up." He makes mention of contributions he made to May's chapel, Gap church, Barnett's church, and others. Here's another item: "I subscribed, I think, at Zion church, perhaps or some other church for missionary causes—foreign and domestic, $5. Pay it up. Amen." And another: "I paid 50 cents for the support of the Gospel. Borrowed it from Aurelius. Paid him up."

Out of the abundance of his heart he gave to God's causes, and God always took cognizance of his contributions for the means were always provided in some manner to make good the obligation.

Brother Sheffey never forgot a promise. His diary and letters reveal the fact that his pledges were just as binding as a bond would make them. Here is a letter in which we see something of his high regard for a promise made to a colored woman. It is a revelation of his love for all of God's creatures. The letter was addressed to a number of friends at White Gate, in Giles county. It follows:

"This is a sweet and lovely evening—April 26, 1897. I am now at or near Richlands P. O., Tazewell county, Va. This letter is from your sweet friend, Robert S. Sheffey. The commencement of the 24th of this month, about 7 months ago, my wife died after 12 o'clock in the night, and I have been working, and traveling, and preaching, and visiting more than common. I have been out from home right smart while ever since I saw you all last as I came through your part of the world. . . . The reason, partly, I write now is because I want you to attend to a little business for me. I saw a colored woman near Brother William Wrights. She lives south from Brother Wrights, perhaps near the creek over there somewhere. I promised our sweet Lord to spare her $1.00 to get one dollar's worth of calico to make her some clothes. She will remember it if you see her or send her word. I enclose the amount in the letter. Her name to the best of my recollection is Emiline or Angeline Ratliff. She married a colored man—nearly white or red. Mr. George Fanning would know him and perhaps Mr. Barbee. Get the calico at Dublin Depot at 5 cts. a yard if you go over there or get it at Mr. Barbees at 5 cts. a yard or at Mr. Banes at 5 cts. a yard. It will get 20 yards. Get the calico. I would rather she would not get the money for fear she would spend it for something else. Keep count of the yards and the price.... I have been trying to fix my little business as I am getting along in years.... I send the one dollar to pay for the calico for Mrs. Ratliff, a colored woman nearly black, and her husband, recollect, is nearly white and perhaps is not as bright in mind as some. Overlook writing so much about it. She seemed at one time to be hard run.... Meeting has been going on here about 2 weeks.... I have been in meetings at other places over on Clear Fork, at Graham, in Baptist Valley, on or near Indian Creek, in the Cecil neighborhood, at town of Jeffersonville. I have preached, sung, and prayed in secret a many a time and prayed in families and in public a many time since I saw you. The people have been very kind to me and my animal certainly. Spared me money at different times. I had to get clothes of different kinds and got some socks too. Glory to God and the Lamb."

Diction didn't mean much to the old preacher. He did not know much about punctuation and the proper phrasing of sentences, but there is one thing he did know and that was God. His letters were always expressive of the love he had in his heart for all humanity. It made no difference to him as to how he expressed himself. God knew and that was enough for him.

Among the spots infrequently visited by Rev. Sheffey was the Rehoboth Methodist church, near Union, in Monroe county, W. Va. The major part of Sheffey's ministry was confined to those counties adjacent to Giles county, in Southwestern Virginia. However, inquiry has developed the fact that this itinerant preacher occasionally visited Monroe county, particularly that section about Rehoboth church. This church is located approximately thirty-five miles from where Sheffey lived while a resident of Giles county. This was a favorite gathering place for the Methodists of Southern West Virginia and parts of Virginia many years ago and precious memories cluster about it even to this late day.

The Rehoboth Methodist church has one of the most

interesting histories of all churches in Methodism. It is said to be the oldest Protestant church in America still in use. I do not know that this is true but I have heard the statement a number of times. A recent visit to this old church proved to be most interesting to the writer. The building stands about two miles southeast of Union, the county seat of Monroe county. It is about a quarter of a mile off the main highway, the site designated by a marker which reads: "Rehoboth Church—Indians were still about when Rehoboth church was dedicated by Bishop Asbury in 1786, and rifles were carried by the worshippers. This is the oldest church building west of the Allegheny mountains."

The church is a log structure. It has been rebuilt in recent years, but many of the original logs are to be seen in the walls of the building. The seats are made out of huge trees split open and holes bored in either ends for legs upon which the hewed timbers rest. No windows are in the building and only one door. A balcony extends across the end and on either side facing the pulpit which is an elevated affair in the end of the building. The original building has been completely covered over with a tin roof which insures a good state of preservation for many years to come.

Upon the occasion of our last visit to this old house of worship we found a number of old records showing that people from almost every section of this nation have at some time or other sought out this place and left their names and addresses upon these ledgers which have been left there for that purpose.

Over the door may be seen a bronze tablet bearing the inscription: "Rehoboth—Oldest church building west of the Allegheny mountains. Society of Methodists, organized 1784. First Bishop of Methodism Francis Asbury was present at the raising of the church 1785. Dedicated this log-meeting house 1786, and held three Annual Conferences, May 1792—1793-1796. The church was built chiefly by the means of and through the industry of Edward Keenan, who deeded for church and burying grounds five acres for 'as long as grass grows and water flows.' Restored in 1927 under supervision of Rev. George W. Richardson, Presiding Elder. August 31, 1930."

Edward Keenan, the builder of this church, lies buried within fifteen feet of the north-east corner of the structure, and on his simple tombstone one reads these words: "Edward Keenan, born 1742; died August 1, 1826. He built Rehoboth church and gave the lot of ground."

Each year a special service is held at the old church which is attended by great multitudes of people. Some of the outstanding preachers of Methodism have been called upon to occupy the pulpit during these services. In 1939 Bishop Adna W. Leonard was the visiting preacher. Other bishops of the church have participated in these yearly meetings.

Chapter X

Edward Fleming Sheffey

The story of the life of Robert Sayers Sheffey would not be complete without telling the essential facts in the life of Edward Fleming Sheffey, his son. "Eddy," the familiar name by which Brother Sheffey called his son, was for almost fifty years connected with the business, civic, educational, and church activities of the "Hill City." It is safe to say that no factor touching his life was more important in the building of his most excellent character than that of his sainted father and mother. We see that influence reaching across the years of his full life and even on into the lives of his children. The full weight of his life and his Christian influence upon the religious life of his adopted city as well as upon the lives of his children remains for an eternity to reveal.

Edward Sheffey was born November 12, 1865, at Trigg, Giles county, Virginia, and died on January 10, 1933 in Lynchburg. He was 67 years of age. He was married to Miss Mattie Elizabeth Mahood, member of a prominent family in Lynchburg, on December 10, 1890. Her death occurred on April 25, 1927.

Six sons and one daughter, grown to maturity, were the fruits of this marriage. One daughter, Elizabeth Helen Sheffey, died a few weeks after birth.

Robert A. Sheffey, educated at Randolph-Macon College, Ashland, Va., and Cornell University, Ithaca, N. Y., is a well known architect in the city of Bluefield, W. Va. He was a member of the A. E. F., France 1918-19, and while engaged in military service studied architecture with the Sorbonne Detachment, A. E. F., Paris, in 1919.

Edward F. Sheffey, II, was educated at Randolph-Macon College, Washington & Lee University, University of Virginia, and Harvard University. He also saw service overseas with the A. E. F., in France. After his return he was associated with the Department of Labor in Washington City.

Charles Phillips Mahood Sheffey received his education at Randolph-Macon College, and Johns-Hopkins University. For two years he was a teacher at Randolph-Macon Academy, Bedford, Va. He has served several years as a medical missionary of the Methodist church at Lusambo, Belgian Congo. He went to the Congo in 1922, and was placed in charge of the medical work at Wembo Nyama and over the adjacent district. The Board of Missions issued a periodical giving the history of its missionaries and in this brief sketch said that Dr. Sheffey "took care of hundreds of hospital patients each year and gave thousands of treatments in the dispensaries" and added that he was "most active in evangelistic work among the hospital patients."

John M. Sheffey received his education at Randolph-Macon College and Harvard University and at the time this story was written was a lawyer identified with the Tri-Continental Corporation on Wall Street, N. Y. City.

Coke Smith Sheffey was educated at Randolph-Macon College and the University of Chicago. He associated himself with the well-known firm of Quinn-Marshall Co., Inc., in Lynchburg. It will be observed that he is a namesake of Dr. A. Coke Smith, a bishop of the Methodist church, who was pastor of the Court Street Methodist Church in Lynchburg in 1895-1899.

Max Sheffey did not attend any higher educational institution. But for many years he was associated with the Guggenheimer, Inc., store in Lynchburg as an efficient salesman.

Miss Grace Sheffey received degrees from the Randolph-Macon Women's College in Lynchburg and William & Mary College. She identified herself with the Methodist Orphanage in Richmond.

Much of the information which follows is gleaned from "The Lynchburg News" and was published at the time of the death of Edward Sheffey. Among other things it says:

"Edward Sheffey was educated in the public and private schools of Giles county and the first position he ever held was on the Pearisburg, Virginian, before he was sixteen years old. When he first came to Lynchburg from Pearisburg, he was with Nowlin Brothers, wholesale grocers. Later he joined the firm of Guggenheimer Co., wholesale dry goods, later becoming vice-president and secretary. He left that concern in 1904 to join Craddock-Terry Company.

"Mr. Sheffey had been secretary-treasurer, credit manager and a director of Craddock-Terry Company. He was a member of the board of trustees of the Randolph-Macon system of colleges and schools and chairman of the executive committee of Randolph-Macon Woman's College. he also served as a member of the Lynchburg school board. He had held several official positions in Court Street Methodist Church and was superintendent of the Sunday School from 1891 to 1927—36 years.

"He was a member of the board of aldermen from 1915 to 1920, being president of that body at the time the bicameral council gave way to the present form of government. He was very active for years on behalf of the Y. M. C. A. and the Anti-Saloon League, and was a director of the National and Lynchburg Credit Men's Association. At one time he was a member of the Sunday School board of the Virginia Methodist Conferencce and was vice-president of the Virginia State Sunday School Association from 1911 to 1916. He was president of the Y. M. C. A. for a considerable time. In 1924 he was a member of the extension committee of the International Lions Club, being a charter member of the Lynchburg club. He was also affiliated with the Masons, Odd Fellows and Junior Order of the United American Mechanics."

An editorial appearing in that same paper on January 11, 1933, the day after his death had this to say of Edward Fleming Sheffey:

"It can be said of Edward F. Sheffey that there was not a phase of community activity in which he was not interested and few in which he did not take an active part. In church, in business, in education, in charity, and welfare work, in fraternities, and in politics he was prominently allied with some agency. There was nothing perfunctory in his allegiance to any cause or to any movement. Once engaged in any enterprise he was aggressively, enthusiastically committed and aggressively, enthusiastically, systematically and energetically at work. Calm and unruffled, even deliberate in his movements, he radiated energy, was unrelenting in his devotion to the work at hand, always pressing ahead and always urging on his fellow-workers.

"To recount some of the activities of this human dynamo is to give an idea of the extent of his work in the community he had made his home since coming out of the southwest fifty years ago. He was superintendent for 36 years of the Sunday School at Court Street Methodist Church with which he affiliated himself soon after his arrival. He was a member of the board of stewards. He was a member of the Sunday School board of the Virginia Sunday School Association. In all that time his attendance at church service was regular and his work unremitting. He was active in work for the Young Men's Christian Association, serving as director and president for many years. He was on the board of the Randolph-Macon system of colleges and chairman of the executive board of Randolph-Macon Woman's College. He was actively interested in public schools and in their development."

"The religious and educational work of Mr. Sheffey is mentioned first because that is the way he appraised the relative importance of his activities. But in business he was just as active and just as efficient and as tireless in his application. First associated with a wholesale grocery and then a wholesale dry goods house, in which he held high position, he became later affiliated with Craddock-Terry Company, where he remained during the last thirty years of his life, becoming secretary-treasurer and credit manager for that firm. His coworkers in that firm testify to his zest, to his efficiency.

"His other activities can but be sketched. Member of the city council for five years, during part of which time he was president of the board of alderman, he worked in public affairs as in church and business. He served as member of the executive committee of the Virginia Anti-Saloon League, as director of the National Credit Men's Association, as member of committees of Lions International and was member of the Masonic order, of the Odd Fellows, the Junior Order of American Mechanics and Oakwood Country Club.

"In the course of a long and active life Mr. Sheffey

made many friends and some enemies and few were lukewarm. He was not a man to make lukewarm attachments or indifferent opponents. But it may be said, that while he kept his friends, animosities did not persist. When he died old enmities had died, but old friendships had had rebirth."

The funeral services for Edward F. Sheffey were conducted from the Court Street Methodist church in Lynchburg on January 11, 1933. Burial was in Spring Hill cemetery in that city. Attending the funeral were representatives of the board of stewards of Court Street church; board of trustees of Randloph-Macon system of colleges and schools; Randolph-Macon Woman's College faculty and students; Craddock-Terry Company; the Lions Club and the Junior Order of United American Mechanics. Among the active and honorary pallbearers may be found the names of many of the outstanding citizens of Lynchburg.

No more effective monument to the memory of this man is to be found in the city of Lynchburg today than that of the impress of his life upon the religious forces of his adopted city. For more than forty years he gave his energies to the building of the master's Kingdom. He was closely associated with every Christian influence in the city. In 1899 he was chairman of the building committee which erected the beautiful church that is now the home of the Court Street Methodist congregation. He assisted in the canvas of the membership of the church for subscriptions to the project. Associated with him was the Hon. Carter Glass, later a United States Senator.

As superintendent of the Sunday School at Court Street church his work was outstanding among all the churches of the Virginia conference. Through his labors the school obtained a select library of 1600 volumes. His motto for his school was: "All the church in the Sunday School. All the Sunday School in the church. All for Christ." His aim: "Every member a Christian; every Christian a worker; every worker trained." This Sunday School was the pride of his heart. Upon one occasion he conducted the entire school on an excursion to Niagara Falls. A newspaper article, dated September 14, 1899, carried a two column length article telling the story of the trip. It required two long trains to carry the huge crowd. This was the culmination of a "vision of the seer of the Lynchburg Court Methodist Sunday School." For years he published a monthly bulletin for his school which was indeed a very creditable piece of work for a man whose hands were already busily engaged in the work of the commercial world.

Edward Sheffey was a very thoughtful parent. He always found time to acquaint himself with the problems of his children and at certain seasons of the year he would remember them with a long letter. I have one before me written at the beginning of the New Year, dated just a few brief days prior to his death. These letters were full of Christian faith and God-like admonition. This letter closes with these words: "Saturday night a wonderful watch night service from London was heard over the radio. A great preacher read the Scriptures, the choir sang, and the preacher spoke, all in fifteen minutes, and at midnight in London 'Big Ben' on the Parliament tower tolled out the old, rang in the new year. We also heard the chimes of Riverside church in New York ring in the New Year in America. God grant that it may be a new year of courage, faith, hope and real success in every way possible to everyone receiving this and all others in the world around and that at the close of the year it may be possible for those then surviving to say 'God is in His heaven and all is well with the world' ". That was the last year of the life of Edward Sheffey, but today he lives in God's Heaven and all is well with his soul.

He liked to remember his friends with Christmas cards at the Yuletide season. One of them reads:

> "If you and I—just you and I—
> Should laugh instead of worry;
> If we should grow—just you and I—
> Kinder and sweeter-hearted,
>
> Perhaps in some near by and by
> A good time might get started;
> Then what a happy world 'twould be
> For you and me—for you and me!"

"And may Christmas joys be yours. May the New Year be a happy one to you; happy to many more whose happiness depends on you. So may each year be happier than the last. God bless you! Faithfully yours, Edward F. Sheffey."

Being advised of the expected advent of a child into the home of one of his sons, he wrote the following letter which shows something of the tender affection he had for his children. It is the voice of his own father, the sainted Robert Sayers Sheffey, speaking in words indicative of love and interest. The letter follows:

"How good, great, thoughtful, all-powerful and loving God is! Truly He loves with an everlasting love and will 'never leave us nor forsake us.' Surely, if there ever was a man who has had an unmistakable evidence of God's abiding, over-ruling love and care I am that man! 'Bless the Lord, O my soul, and all that is within me, bless His holy name!

"I have just read over the first chapter of Luke. What a wonderful chapter it is. You can well imagine the reason I turned at this special time to this lovely human-divine chapter. Truly, the conception, birth, and life of a dear child is one of the greatest and most profound of all the miracles of the universe. And it is through such miracles—hundreds, thousands, millions of them—that the human family is kept from disappearing from the earth, names of families are preserved and the great work of the world carried out.

"I thank you for writing me of the prospective heir to the house of Sheffey! Fine! I had been in doors about a week yesterday when your most welcome letter came. I told mother it brought the best news I had had for quite a while! The best I ever had along that line. And it is great that the dear prospective mother is well, cheerful, happy! Fine! I am sure the sunny disposition of our dear children, beginning with your dear self, on down—Charles, Max—all, is due in great measure to the happy, joyous mother of them all!

"I congratulate you both most heartily. You are now on the way to real lasting, honest-to-goodness happiness. With home, wife, child, God and man's needs and highest desires may be met.

"Already I have prayed and I shall aim to pray daily the power of the Highest may over-shadow dear _____, keep her in reasonable strength and health."

Edward Fleming Sheffey had the same kind of faith in God that his revered father, Robert Sayers Sheffey, possessed. They saw God alike. Their spirits were akin in every respect. It would be safe to say of Edward Sheffey, as it is of his father, that nothing was attempted, nothing undertaken, until God had been contacted. It is no wonder that "Eddy" Sheffey became a great and a good man. His character was laid in the same kind of mould as was that of his father. It is an interesting thing to note that he would often write to his father asking that he pray for the success of the business in which he was engaged. And he would always suggest that he be advised that this was being done. In one letter he said that his concern had had a wonderful year in their business and all this he attributed to the fact that God had answered prayer.

Charles Phillips Mahood Sheffey wore that same kind of mantle out yonder in darkest Africa—the mantle that fell from the sainted grandfather and beloved father. In the name of the Master, the Methodist Church proudly boasts of the service he rendered and the services of the other members of the Sheffey household.

We append an article which appeared in "The Lynchburg News" on September 2, 1922, relative to the departure of Charles Sheffey for Africa: "Dr. Charles Phillips Mahood Sheffey of Court Street Methodist Church, Lynchburg, Va., under appointment as Medical Missionary to the Belgian Congo, Africa, August 1, 1922, by Bishop Cannon, Jr., sailed from New York August 19th for Antwerp. A cablegram was received from Dr. Sheffey August 31st from Brussels indicating he had arrived and was safe and well and that connection would be made at Antwerp with boat sailing for the East Coast of Africa August 31st. On September 2nd, a cablegram came from Brussels signed by Bishop James Cannon, Jr., and Dr. E. H. Rawlings, Foreign Missionary Secretary of the Methodist Episcopal Church, South, expressing their gratitude that Dr. Sheffey had given himself to the service, adding that 'he left today enthusiastic concerning work.'

"A letter written by Dr. Sheffey on board the Kroonland, soon after she sailed August 9th, which letter was sent back by the pilot, expressed his great appreciation of the many kindnesses shown him, especially for the five packages of mail, a large packet from the Mission Board at Nashville, scores of letters and many telegrams. He added, 'I am unafraid as I go out and I know we each one are unafraid as we go to our duties. We have the consolation of duty well done. At least that is our hope, each one in his own work. I shall be remembering, praying, loving, and that bridges all things—space and time. My love to all who have been so kind. I can only thank them from the bottom of my heart and that seems so little.'

"Dr. Sheffey's financial support is being provided for as a 'special' by the Epworth Leaguers of the Memphis Conference, M. E. Church, South, of which Mr. W. R. Brown, ministerial student at Trinity College, Durham, N. C., is secretary. It is known that Dr. Sheffey greatly regretted his inability to visit some of the chapters of the Memphis Leagues. This was impossible because of the urgent call to go to Wembo Nyama to render every service in his power to not only the natives but our missionaries as well, they being without the service of a physician since Dr. D. R. Mumpower the consecrated and devoted founder of the Mission work there, was compelled to return to the United States, on account of the illness of Mrs. Mumpower. Dr. Sheffey is very grateful to the Leaguers and the kind friends for their abiding prayers. He earnestly covets an interest in the prayers of all believers in missions that God may use him not only in his efforts to heal the bodies of men, women and little children of the Dark Continent, but as he seeks to impart to them some knowledge of the Christ who came that they might 'see great light.'

"On the walls of his home Sunday School, the boys' and girls' World club of Court Street church last Sunday placed his picture along-side that of his Sunday School class-mate and life-time friend, Frank J. Gilliam, who for almost two years has been missionary in the Belgian Congo. They were both members of the Sunday School class for years taught by Mr. E. L. Bell, former superintendent and later for years teacher in Court Street Sunday School.

"Farewell receptions were tendered Dr. Sheffey by the board of stewards and the missionary societies of Court

Street a short time before he left for New York to which point he was accompanied by his parents, Mr. and Mrs. Edward F. Sheffey, his sister, Miss grace S. Sheffey, and five brothers, Robert A., Edward F., II. Max Hugh, John Mahood and Coke Smith Sheffey, all of whom were privileged to accompany him to the boat and bid him Godspeed in his life's work."

From "Who's Who in America" we quote: "Edward Fleming Sheffey, shoe manufacturer, was born in Giles county, Virginia, Nov. 12, 1865, son of Rev. Robert Sayers Sheffey, evangelist, and Eliza Wagoner Stafford Sheffey; educated public and private schools; married Mattie Elizabeth Mahood, of Lynchburg, Va., Dec. 10, 1890; with Guggenheimer & Co., wholesale dry goods, Lynchburg, 1882-1904, becoming vice-president, secretary and treasurer; with Craddock-Terry Co., since October 1, 1904, now secretary and treasurer and director; president Old Dominion Box Co.; member Common Council, Lynchburg; member Board of Trustees Randolph-Macon College; chairman executive committee Randolph-Macon Woman's College. Democrat. Member M. E. Church, South; superintendent Court Street Church Sunday School since 1891; member Sunday School Board Virginia Conference; member executive committee Lynchburg Anti-Saloon League; member Lynchburg Y. M. C. A., director and ex-president; vice-president Virginia State Sunday School Association; director National Association Credit Men, 1914. Mason. Home, No. 922, Floyd Street. Office, 50 Ninth Street, Lynchburg, Va."

Chapter XI

The Old Fashioned Camp Meeting

No history of Robert Sayers Sheffey would be complete without a chapter on the old-fashioned camp meeting which was in full flower in this hill country at the time of his most active ministry. He "loved the brethren" and wherever they were assembled it was his greatest delight to join with them in the religious upheavals which swept those areas where these meetings were held. In many instances these meetings were far-reaching in scope of territory touched. They were not merely community-wide affairs. People traveled great distances to attend them and to share in the spiritual blessings that came to the worshippers.

Brother Sheffey was at home in these meetings. Singing and praying and preaching and shouting were elemental in his life. In this atmosphere he "moved, and lived, and had his being." In one of the histories reciting the fact of his "second birth" it is recorded that this experience took place at the old Cripple Creek camp ground in Wythe county, Va. However, men who have heard him tell the story of his conversion say that the "heart warming" took place in a service being held over Greenway's store, in Abingdon, Va., but no matter where it occurred he was always certain that it had taken place. And in the camp meeting he found a constant source of joy; it was one of the delightful experiences of his life and he eagerly attended them and participated in the services from day to day.

The early growth of Methodism is in a large measure attributable to the old-fashioned camp meetings which began about the turn of the century. The Presbyterian and Baptist churches also shared largely in the results of these meetings. Denominational differences were forgotten in these meetings and men labored together to the end that His Kingdom might come and His will be done in the lives of those who attended the services.

Francis Asbury, the apostle of American Methodism, thought well of the camp meeting as a means of spiritual grace. He eagerly seized upon this potent agency as a means of extending the Kingdom. As early as 1802 he wrote: "I think well of large meetings, camp and quarterly meetings. The more preachers to preach and pray, and so many of God's people, and so many people that need conversion, and so many of the children of God's children present, we may hope for great things in the nature of things."

Many historians have attempted to gauge the results of these meetings. Some have written of them with a feeling of approbation. Others have been quite critical in their estimates of the good accomplished. But the fact remains that there was unusual evidence of spiritual power in the old-fashioned camp meeting. The fact also remains that hundreds and thousands of men, women, and children, have experienced striking reformations in their personal lives. The further fact remains that certain communities feeling the impact of these great spiritual meetings have produced some of the greatest religious characters that this country has known in a hundred years or more. At this late day it is quite noticeable that the communities where these meetings were held more than a half century ago remain as a genuine stronghold for God and His righteousness.

Men are powerless to gauge the works of the Almighty. His infinite power to work and achieve transcends the ability of finite minds to know and understand.

> "God moves in a mysterious way,
> His wonders to perform."

" 'Tis done, the great transaction's done," and men stand in wonderment and awe! Pentecostal power is the only explanation of these great religious awakenings. "God's people are a peculiar people" and redeemed souls are awakened souls, always bear the stamp of an awakened conscience which has been made alive unto God.

The camp meeting is believed to have resulted from the joint services conducted by two brothers, John and Thomas McGee, the first a member of the Methodist church, the latter a member of the Presbyterian faith. John McGee was one of the pioneers of American Methodism.

His contemporaries were the men who planted the foundation stones of Methodism on the American continent.

These brothers were abundant in labors in lower Kentucky during the years 1799 and 1800. For a time their labors were largely confined to Logan and Christian counties in that state. Large groups of people came to hear them preach and became interested in the work they were doing. The magnitude of their work reached such proportions that no church building could house the crowds. When summer came they decided to move out into the woods and here they erected an altar and began to preach. A. G. Meacham in his "Compendious History of the Rise and Progress of the Methodist Church in America" says: "The people in order to accommodate themselves, carried provisions for their families and beasts, in their wagons; erected tents, and continued some days in the exercise of singing, praying, and preaching. Thus commenced what has since received the appellation of "Camp Meetings'; a revival of the 'Feast of Tabernacles.' " He further adds: "The number that attended them is almost incredible to tell. When collected on the ground, and whilst the meetings continued, such crowds would be passing and re-passing, that the roads, paths and woods appeared to be literally strewed with people! Whole settlements and neighborhoods would appear to be vacated and such was the draught from them, that it was only here and there that a solitary house would contain an aged house-keeper; young and old very generally pressing through every difficulty to see the Camp Meeting!"

John McGee gives a very terse account of one of the first of these meetings. His description follows:

"We loved, and prayed, and preached together; and God was pleased to own and bless us and our labors. In the year 1799 we agreed to make a tour through the Barrens, toward Ohio, and concluded to attend a sacramental solemnity in the Rev. Mr. McGready's congregation, on Red River, in our way. When we came there I was introduced by my brother, and received an invitation to address the congregation from the pulpit; and I know not that God ever favored me with more light and liberty than he did each day while I endeavored to convince the people they were sinners, and urged the necessity of repentance, and of a change from nature to grace, and held up to their view the greatness, freeness, and fullness of salvation, which was in Christ Jesus, for lost, guilty, condemned sinners. My brother and the Rev. Mr. Hodge preached with much animation and liberty. The people felt the force of truth, and tears ran down their cheeks; but all was silent until Monday, the last day of the feast. Mr. Hodge gave a useful discourse; an intermission was given, and I was appointed to preach. While Mr. Hodge was preaching a woman in the east end of the house got an uncommon blessing, broke through order, and shouted for some time, and then sat down in silence. At the close of the sermon Messrs. Hodge, McGready, and Rankin went out of the house; my brother and myself sat still; the people seemed to have no disposition to leave their seats. My brother felt such a power come over him that he quit his seat and sat down on the floor of the pulpit, I suppose not knowing what he did. A power which caused me to tremble was upon me. There was a solemn weeping all over the house. Having a wish to preach, I strove against my feelings; at length I rose up and told the people I was appointed to preach, but there was a greater than I preaching, and exhorted them to let the Lord God Omnipotent reign in their hearts, and to submit to him, and their souls should live. Many broke silence; the woman in the east end of the house shouted tremendously. I left the pulpit to go to her, and as I went along through the people it was suggested to me, 'You know these people are much for order, they will not bear this confusion; go back and be quiet.' I turned to go back, and was near falling. The power of God was strong upon me; I turned again, and losing sight of the fear of man, I went through the house shouting and exhorting with all possible ecstasy and energy, and the floor was soon covered with the slain. Their cries for mercy pierced the heavens, and mercy came down. Some found forgiveness, and many went away from the meeting feeling unutterable agonies of soul for redemption in the blood of Jesus. This was the beginning of that glorious revival in this country which was so great a blessing to thousands; and from this meeting camp meetings took their rise. One man, for want of horses for all his family to ride and attend the meeting, fixed up his wagon, in which he took them and his provisions, and lived on the ground throughout the meeting. He had left his worldly cares behind him, and had nothing to do but attend on divine services.

"The next meeting was a Camp Meeting. A number of wagons loaded with people came together and camped on the ground, and the Lord was present and approved of their zeal by sealing a pardon to about forty souls. The next camp meeting was on the Ridge, where there was an increase of people, and carriages of different descriptions, and a great many preachers of the Presbyterian and Methodist orders, and some of the Baptist—but the latter were generally opposed to the work. Preaching commenced, and the people prayed, and the power of God attended. The nights were truly awful. The camp ground was well illuminated; the people were differently exercised —some exhorting, some shouting, some praying, and some crying for mercy, while others lay as dead men on the ground. At this meeting it was computed that 100 souls were converted. But perhaps the greatest meeting we ever witnessed in this country took place shortly after, on Desha's Creek, near Cumberland River. Many thousands of people attended. The mighty power and mercy of God were manifested. The people fell before the word like corn before a storm of wind, and many rose from the dust with divine glory shining in their countenances, and gave glory to God in such strains as made the hearts of stubborn sinners to tremble; and after the first gust of praise, they would break forth in volleys of exhortation."

Sheffey always attended these meetings if it was at all possible for him to do so. And most of the preachers were glad to see him coming for they knew how effective he was in prayer. Sheffey could start a revival like no other preacher of his day because of his unusual power in prayer. He would pray for hours until he had received the answer to his prayers and then the meeting would break forth on the right and the left in great religious demonstrations. The tides of religious fervor would roll over the great congregations like the tidal waves of the seas.

In one community where a meeting of this nature was

being held Sheffey appeared upon the scene rather unexpectedly. He was called upon to pray, but the skies apparently were deaf to his prayers and God did not answer. The next day he went out into the woods and remained in prayer until long after twelve o'clock. There had been preaching but no conviction had come upon the congregation. A young preacher who did not know Sheffey very well had preached at the morning service. At the next service Sheffey was called upon again to pray and he prayed for the "old devil and the little devil." The young preacher did not understand and so he asked some of the other "brethren" why Sheffey had prayed such a prayer. They advised him to ask Sheffey. He called the old saint into his tent, and, in the presence of some of the other preachers, asked him what he meant by praying for the devil. Sheffey quaintly said, "Young man, there are some things you know, and some things you do not know. You know when Columbus discovered America, but you don't know why he discovered America." That was the only answer he gave. He did not tell the young brother why he prayed for "the Lord to put a chunk of ice under the devil's tail and send him hell-ward."

The Wabash camp meeting, in Giles county, was one of the high spots on Sheffey's "circuit." The site of this old camp ground was originally located on the property owned by the Eaton family. It is now a part of the estate owned by Shuler K. Johnson. It was established about the year 1834.

Dr. Price in his "History of Holston Methodism" records a letter from Edward Johnson, a venerable citizen of Giles county, addressed to Dr. Cunningham, and written from Poplar Hill, Va., on February 4, 1875, in which he says:

"The first camp ground in this country was built about the year 1809 or 1810. It was known as Chinquapin Camp Ground. The next one built was at Mechanicsburg, now in Bland county, about the year 1813. In 1819 or 1820 a cloth tent meeting was held about two miles west of Poplar Hill. In 1822 or 1823 another camp ground was built near the old Chinquapin Camp Ground. The last meeting there was held in 1833 by Revs. Daniel B. Carter and Hugh Johnson. After the close of this meeting, ground was bought at

Wabash and a camp ground established there, where it has remained ever since.

The influence of the Wabash camp meeting continues to be felt in this country even at this late day. A number of people who are members of the Methodist churches throughout Southwestern Virginia and Southern West Virginia owe their religious experiences to the influences of those great revivals which were the outgrowth of these unusual meetings. Charles W. Kelly, member of the Holston Conference for more than half a century, and who died in Knoxville in the year 1939, was a product of this camp meeting influence. Glenn G. Martin, of the Baltimore conference, and Wm. Stuart Martin, Methodist preacher in Pennsylvania for many years, were also members of families resident in this area at the time of these camp meetings. It is interesting to note that their mothers were sisters and aunts of Robert S. Sheffey's wife. Another preacher of this area is Monroe E. Stafford, son of J. R. Stafford, and member of the West Virginia conference. A son, Garland Stafford, (son of Monroe), is a member of the Western North Carolina conference. Hugh S. Johnson, late member of the Holston conference, and Steward Munsey, of the West Virginia conference, were born and reared near the site of the Wabash campground.

Another campground near the Wabash meeting place was called Hoge's Camp Ground. This campground was not in existence for many years, probably three or four years at most. It is said that at one meeting there were more than one hundred and fifty conversions.

Dr. Price tells the following interesting story in his history of Holston Methodism of the origin of the name "Wabash" as applied to the campground: "A son of Mr. James Evans, who resided on Kimberling creek, had recently moved to Indiana and settled on Wabash river, where he succeeded in making a comfortable fortune. He persuaded his father to emigrate to that place. He started, but his wagon broke down at the end of the first or second day's drive, and he stopped for a time in a cabin that had been built by some hunters. Winter setting in before he was ready to proceed on his jounery, he remained in the cabin for the winter. David Brown wittily remarked to his brother William: "Well Billy, Evans has got to his Wabash already." The name thus given in irony to the place and the little stream at the place still adheres to them."

The Kimberling campground was another popular meeting place in those historic days of the religious groups of this section. It was situated on Kimberling Creek and was established about the year 1850. It was here that William E. Munsey, the flaming torch-bearer of the Master, was converted under the touch of George Stewart, pastor on the adjacent charge. Stewart observed Munsey at one of the services and saw that he was deeply convicted of sin. He approached him and through his assistance Munsey was led to the altar and to God. Munsey was then about 16 years of age. With the passing of the years he became one of the most effective ministers in all Methodism. He served churches in a number of the large cities and drew large crowds who sat spell bound as they listened to his word-paintings of Scriptural truth. His mental powers were extraordinary. He had wisdom infinitely beyond that of the average preacher of his day. His oratory and his eloquence were marveled at by men of God everywhere. He read books and he observed nature, he delved deeply into the hidden realms of every subject upon which he attempted to preach. It is said that he would spend whole nights in research work all unconscious of the passing of the hours. The story is told of him that he went to spend the night in a certain home and when he was escorted up to his room by his host to retire he discovered a book which dealt with some subject in which he was vitally interested. Munsey sat down and began to read. He kept on reading and the breaking of day found him still poring away at its pages. His host came up to awaken him and discovered that he had not even thought of retiring. When the man of the house called, Munsey said, "What time is it?"

Munsey was a member of the well-known Bland county family of that name. More than one member of this family has been noted for oratorical ability and forensic power. Thomas J. Munsey, one-time candidate of the Republican party in Virginia for the governorship, was known throughout the length and the breadth of the old commonwealth as an eloquent speaker and orator of no mean ability.

It was at the Kimberling campground that Eliza W. Sheffey's mother, Margaret Wagoner, was converted. "Jimmy" Stafford had gone up to the meeting from his home in the "Irish Settlement." He observed Margaret Wagoner at the altar. He became attracted to her and remarked to some friend, "That's my wife." The young lady was converted at this service. And here also began an acquaintance with "Jimmy" Stafford which ripened into a lovely courtship and was consummated at the altar a few years later. She was a lovely Christian character. She was never perturbed or excited in soul. At the ripe old age of 92 years she closed her eyes to earthly scenes and went away. Her last audible words were caught by her son, Dr. D. H. Stafford, as he sat by her bedside. She had caught a vision of the eternal world and its inhabitants. She said: "Do you see them? I see Jimmy and my Saviour." That's the kind of mother that Elizabeth Stafford Sheffey knew and enjoyed.

Another old campground that enjoyed a wide prestige for a number of years was the Providence camp meeting, near Fries, Virginia, in Grayson county. Many strong and virile Christian characters have been produced by the community surrounding this old camp ground. Wiley J. Phillips, for many years an active and useful member of the Methodist church on the Pacific coast, came from this territory. While resident in Los Angeles he founded "The California Voice," the leading temperance organ of that section. This paper became the mouthpiece of the prohibition forces and led the fight in many a battle for righteousness and sobriety. The Wrights,—Onnie, Bruce, Carl, Carlton—members of the Holston conference, came out of this immediate section. There are many others whose names have added luster and glory to the Kingdom. After a lapse of almost half a century men point with pride to the old camp meetings at Providence, and the influence of those meetings continues to be felt throughout the whole of that territory.

It was in the little Hopewell meeting house, near this campground, that Creed Fulton, the founder of Emory & Henry College, first met the Lord and became a messenger of the Cross and its story of salvation. It is not amiss for us to record that story here for it has never been given to the public in any writing that we have seen.

The story of that conversion is told by Rev. Thomas C. Vaughn, honored local preacher of Holston conference for many years, resident at Spring Valley, Va., when he gave me the story in a brief history of the "Old Grayson Circuit." It came out of the reminiscences of his father, Robert Vaughan, born in the year 1801, an intimate friend of Fulton. The story in his own words follows: "In that Sunday morning talk with my father, he said: 'I remember especially Jessee Green, a polished and spiritual preacher, under whose ministry Fulton was converted. Creed Fulton and myself were intimate friends and companions in our boyhood days, and we took every opportunity we had to hear Jessee Green preach. We were seated together on a Sunday morning in the little Hopewell meeting-house intently listening to a sermon from this consecrated preacher. He used the word "Philanthropist," the meaning of which I did not know, and I touched Fulton's arm so we might remember to discuss it afterwards, but I found the tears were flowing from his eyes. At the close of the sermon Fulton went forward as a penitent and was soon afterwards converted and licensed to exhort. He was a timid and awkward exhorter, but rapidly improved and became one of the great leaders and preachers of our church."

Creed Fulton was born at Summerfield, Grayson county, Virginia, on November 28, 1802. His father was Samuel Fulton, his mother, Martha Jones Fulton. He was one of twelve children. He was licensed to preach at the age of 20 years. His first converts are said to have been members of his own father's household. For 37 years he was an honored member of the traveling connection of the Methodist church.

An interesting story about an incident that happened at the Wabash campground was told to me by the late J. R. Stafford, prominent citizen of Pearisburg, Virginia. It was a gloomy afternoon when the story was recited to the writer, the clouds were hanging low and rain had been falling most of the day. Mr. Stafford recalled that it was a day quite similar when the final service of the camp meeting was about to be held. Brother Sheffey had been very anxious about the service. He wanted the meeting to end in a great gathering of the Christian people and an unusual demonstration of the Holy Spirit. In the afternoon, Mr. Stafford said, he saw Brother Sheffey making his way up to the top of a nearby mountain peak. After the old saint had prayed he arose from his knees and began to walk back and forth clasping his hands together and praising God. He had received an answer to his prayer. In a short time the clouds began to lift and the sun came out in all its glory and the final service of the camp meeting was all that Brother Sheffey could have desired. To talk with God about anything and everything was as natural with Brother Sheffey as for night to follow day.

Great preparations were made for these annual meetings. A letter from the late Rev. J. Tyler Frazier, published in the Pearisburg Virginian in 1893, shows something of the concern manifested by the promoters of these services. It follows: "The Camp Ground Association decided to have a camp meeting at Wabash, August 29th, and preparations are being made to that end. I hope it will be an old-fashioned calico camp meeting. Let it be understood that the people are going to Wabash for religious worship and not for social entertainment. Tent-holders are sometimes over-run by people who come to see, be seen, sleep, eat, entertain company, and be entertained, promenade up and down the road and about the shed. Let these change their habits or stay at home.

"Tent-holders are not hotel keepers. They are there to worship with their families, feed and shelter their invited friends. They may reasonably be expected to care for a real friend from a distance, but not that friend, and one, two, five or more of his friends whom the tent-holders never saw before. Know how your friends are to be provided for before you take them or leave them at home.

"Let it be distinctly understood by all that no huckstering of any kind will be allowed within three miles limit, no picture tents, melon wagons, candy stands, etc., will be allowed. Let all understand this and govern themselves accordingly.

"Let all who love camp meetings help in every way to

preserve good order and promote religious worship. Wear plain clothes. It becomes the occasion and the place.

"Let the prayers, songs and preaching all be done with a view to bring souls to Christ. No preacher is wanted who doesn't come to work. If the tent-holders and friends will co-operate heartily with the preachers the camp meeting will be a success. We hope they will.
"J. T. Frazier."

J. Tyler Frazier was a native of Giles county and was born near the town of Pearisburg, Virginia, and for more than sixty years he was one of the most effective preachers in Holston conference.

Jacob Tyler Frazier was the son of George A. and Sallie Dillon Frazier. He was called the "grand old man of Holston conference." He was a product of the old-fashioned camp meeting having been "born again" at the Old Wabash Camp Ground, in his native county, at the tender age of 16 years. The story has been told that he went to the campground to sell cider and cakes. On one of these visits he was led to Christ, and for 76 years he was a member of the Methodist church. Seventy-one years he was a Methodist preacher. He "died in the 67th year of his admission on trial and in the 65th year of his full membership in the conference," according to the memoir prepared by his friend, Rev. T. J. Eskridge, appearing in the "Holston Annual of 1932." In that same paper, Dr. Eskridge said of this remarkable man: "He towered high above the ordinary both as a preacher and a personality. As a preacher, he was a genius. His insight into scriptural truth was marvelous, and in his presentation of it he swayed multitudes as few men ever have. For years he was the most widely known and admired preacher in his conference. He stirred people to their profoundest depths. While congregations were moved to tears, hardened sinners turned to God and saints were in transports of joy. He had a wonderful flow of language. He was never at a loss for a word. His powers of description were wonderful. He could depict scenes and incidents so vividly that they became visual to the eyes of his hearers. Probably this accounts for the tremendous impression he made at the Centennial session of the Tennessee conference in 1912, in McKendree church, Nashville, when, as the representative of the Holston conference, he made an address on the Old Time Circuit Riders. Quickened by the magic of his words, his audience saw as in a moving panorama, the toils and privations of the evangels of the Cross and their quenchless zeal and all conquering faith as they battled for the Lord."

Chapter XII

The Old-fashioned Camp Meeting

In the story of the old-fashioned camp meeting it is not amiss to give the origin of the "mourner's bench" as the term is used by Methodist people. In these meetings men and women were called to the "mourner's bench" and here multiplied thousands were "born again." I quote from the "Centennial History of American Methodism" written by John Atkinson, D. D., in the year 1884. He says:

"The Mourner's Bench is invested with most sacred associations in American Methodism. At the mourner's bench multitudes found the peace of God. The word 'altar' conveys the same idea in this day, and it is employed in all or nearly all revivals in the Methodist Episcopal Church. The question is of some interest, when and by whom was the practice of inviting awakened persons to the mourner's bench introduced? It is probably not possible to answer that question with certainty. The Rev. Jessee Lee gives, in his Journal, the following record: October 31, 1798, in Virginia, he says: 'At Paup's meeting house Mr. Asbury preached on Eph. v. 25, 26, 27. He gave us a good discourse. Then I exhorted, and the power of the Lord was among us. Many wept and some cried aloud with deep distress. Then Miles Harper exhorted and dismissed the assembly. The class was desired to remain. Brother Mead began to sing, and in a little while many were affected and a general weeping began. John Easter proclaimed aloud, 'I have no doubt but God will convert a soul today.' The preacher then requested all that were under conviction to come together. Several men and women came and fell upon their knees, and the preachers for some time kept singing and exhorting the mourners to expect a blessing from the Lord, till the cries of the mourners became truly awful. Then prayer was made in behalf of the mourners, and two or three found peace." Mr. Boehm witnessed the gathering of penitents at a place or seat to which they were invited as early as about 1800. At a meeting in Delaware, mentioned by the Rev. William Colbert, the mourners were invited 'forward.' Mr. Colbert says: "After love-feast, Brother Cooper preached under the shades from Acts 2:4. Caleb Boyer exhorted after him, but to a restless congregation. He spoke on the subject of a collection that was made. I sang and made some observations on the disorderly behaviour of the congregation and went to prayer. After prayer I called upon the persons in distress to come forward and look to the Lord to convert their souls. Numbers came forward, and repaired to the meeting-house, where we spent some time with them in prayer and left them engaged." This was Sunday, May 24, 1801, in Delaware. Mr. Colbert gives another instance of invitation to penitents on April 18, 1802. The house at St. Martin's he says, "Before we got there was crowded, and a very large number out-of-doors. We fixed a table at the door, and Brother Ryan preached from 1 Peter 2:25. Brother Boehm spoke after him with great power, and after him I spoke. I thought it very remarkable that the people stood so long in the rain to hear the word of God. It continued raining during the public meeting. It kept us back with our love-feast a long time. Seeing no prospect of better weather in a seasonable time, after waiting long, we requested the people to depart that we might hold our love-feast. A blessed time we had. Many spoke feelingly, and a great number of mourners came to join us in prayer when the invitation was given. Glory to God! there was a glorious display of power. Several rose up praising the Lord." The Rev. Henry Smith says: "In looking over my diary I find the following notice: 'Sunday, May 29, 1803, I preached at Front-royal. I met the class, having invited all who wished to serve the Lord to stay with us. Eight or ten did so. After I had spoken to the class I opened a door to receive members into the society. None seemed disposed to join. I then proposed to pray for those who were mourning to know the love of God if they would come forward and kneel down. Eight or ten came."—The venerated Henry Boehm recited these facts to Dr. Johnson for volume referred to in these writings.

It was around the "mourner's bench" and at the sacred altars of Methodism that multiplied thousands of men and women through the years have met with saving grace and the forgiveness of their sins. About these holy places men and women have met with experiences that have changed the whole course of their lives. And even the course of nations and empires have been altered. The "mourner's bench" was very definitely a part of the old-fashioned camp meeting program.

Many and unusual have been the experiences of the participants in the camp meetings which have stretched across much of Methodism in the Eastern part of the United States. Lorenzo Dow tells about them. Peter Cartwright tells about them in his writings. Many men who have written about the early history of Methodism record the tremendous power of God's visitation revealed at these meetings.

One such incident at the Wabash campground has been recounted over and over. Through the kindly assistance of Dr. E. E. Wiley, then pastor of the Trinity Methodist church in Bluefield, W. Va., the writer has received first-hand information from those who were present at the time. I record in full the letters relative to same. The first one is from Dr. J. W. Perry, then pastor of the Abingdon Methodist church, and for more than a half century an honored member of the Holston conference. He writes:

"Your letter has been received. Brother Bailey (W. E.) has given you a very accurate account of the meeting at Wabash. It was an occasion all the way through the time of the camp of intense religious fervor and deep emotion. At almost every gathering there were shouts and hallelujahs. The closing night I had tried to preach from the text in Hebrews 11:14-16: 'For they that say such things declare plainly that they seek a country. And truly, if they had been mindful of that country from whence they came out, they might have had opportunity to have returned. But now they desire a better country, that is, a heavenly: wherefore God is not ashamed to be called their God: for He hath prepared for them a city.' I had tried to be excused for I was not feeling well, and at the close of the sermon I felt completely exhausted. Scores came forward as penitents, and fell down all about the shed. After a little while I went to the preacher's tent and laid down. There was such a tremendous surge of emotion that I, after a time, went back under the shed. All about, penitents were rising with a shout of victory, and many were praising God. They were singing 'Jesus, Lover of My Soul.' As I approached R. A. Kelly, he pointed up toward the roof and said: 'Don't you hear it? The angels are singing.' But I could hear nothing but the volume of the great audience rising in soulful song. A Mrs. Stafford, I was told, felt that she could recognize her mother's voice. Many were looking up, some with index finger pointing up, and their faces were radiant with an almost supernatural light. I have never witnessed such a scene. One was swept into the spirit of the occasion by some irresistible force. I thought that the singing which seemed to come from above in response to those below, was perhaps an echo which could be heard only in certain positions under the shed. Or the atmosphere set in vibration by the immense volume was felt and audible to some sensitive souls. But I do not know, and have never felt disposed to speculate about it. The Spirit of God must have been there making Himself felt in a very marvelous way. It was such an experience as one could never forget. There was something supernatural in the meeting. Of that I have never had any doubt. I remember Frazier, Cobb, R. A. Kelly, C. W. Kelly, and I think A. B. Hunter was there. Brother Bailey, the pastor, was there. Of the others I have no distinct recollection, but rather think that W. N. Wagner may have been present. Following that meeting in the winter I assisted Brother Bailey in a meeting at Poplar Hill. I reached him on Tuesday morning for a service, and about ten young people were converted at the first meeting. Brother Whitley Hicks remarked that was about all we could expect as there were no others in the community. But there were conversions at every service. I left on Saturday, and Bailey closed on Sunday morning, and received fifty-five into the church on profession of faith. I felt that the Wabash meeting had much to do with the results at Poplar Hill."

The second letter comes from Dr. P. L. Cobb, then pastor of the Ridgedale Methodist church in Chattanooga, and a member of the Holston conference since 1892. He writes:

"I have answered your letter several times mentally,

but never in a satisfactory manner. I have never been able to formulate a statement that satisfies my own mind.

"That there was phenomenon, I have no doubt. All the people who were on the right side of the shed were awestruck and excited. The ones who heard it first were on the outside of the shed and evidently called others out that way that they, too, might hear.

"The look on their faces and their manner told the story. All of them, as far as I know, really believed they had been listening to the singing of heavenly beings, they said angels.

"The report spread over the campground and there was general excitement and rejoicing. Everybody was convinced by the earnestness of those who heard the singing.

"I report nothing first hand as I was very busy leading the singing. We were having a great camp meeting and the singing, I thought, was a very important spiritual force. It was the usual camp meeting singing. We were putting all we had into it.

"The important thing to me was that God was there. If there is more rejoicing in Heaven over one sinner that repenteth than over ninety and nine just persons that need no repentance, we know what was going on in Heaven and, if a little of the music spilled over on to the joy under the shed, I am not surprised.

"I thank you for writing, as I have been lured by your kindly approach to make a statement I thought I might never make."

Regarding this same incident, Dr. E. E. Wiley tells how he talked with Rev. W. E. Bailey at his home then on Walton Avenue in Bluefield a few months before his death. At the time of the happening Brother Bailey was pastor of the Staffordsville circuit, near the scene of the incident. Dr. Wiley wrote down the facts as they were given to him and then he asked Brother Bailey to correct any inaccuracies. The account as he gave it follows: The circumstance took place on Monday night, the closing night of the meeting. The following ministers were present: J. Tyler Frazier, R. A. Kelly, W. N. Wagner, P. L. Cobb, J. W. Perry and myself. It was estimated that 5,000 persons were present. A number of penitents had been at the altar and professed conversion. J. T. Frazier was in charge of the after-service, being the presiding elder. Brother Frazier turned to me, during the singing of a hymn, and said, "Ed, start that old hymn, 'Jesus, Lover of My Soul.'" As we started the second stanza of this song, W. N. Wagner called out above the sound of the voices of the congregation, "Listen, listen, the redeemed hosts of heaven are singing. I hear the voice of my mother." I then heard the chorus, softer than human voices but clearly distinguishable through the remainder of the stanza. A thrill came over the audience and many pressed toward the front of the building.

I have already mentioned the old Kimberlin campground in Bland county in these writings. The site of this campground is in the Kimberlin valley where for more than a half century the men and women of that section have recounted the experiences of those old-fashioned meetings and thought upon the tremendous effect for good growing out of these meetings as they have related themselves to the people of that section of Bland county. A most interesting letter from Dr. J. A. Wagner, of Bland, Va., reveals that he was born on Kimberlin in the same year that Bland county was formed. He spent his boyhood and early manhood among the people of that section, and has been a medical practitioner in the homes of the people for many years. Quite naturally he has known them in a very intimate way. He says of them in this letter written a few years ago that "They were practically all farmers, and had to work hard from early morning till dewy eve to keep the wolf from the door. They did not have hours of leisure as we have, no time to play or attend ball games, no bridge or card parties of any kind, no clubs or lodges for the fathers or mothers to attend at night, but when bedtime came, a chapter of Scripture was read, many times by the children, and all would kneel in prayer to Almighty God and be led by the father and mother.

"I do not want to try to estimate the amount of good that was done, but I do know that no child that was trained in that way will ever forget it.

"What I really want to say is this: 'I do not believe any valley in Bland county or any adjoining county has produced more preachers than Kimberlin.' Dr. John Miller and the Rev. F. F. Repass both lived and preached on Kimberlin, but were not born there. The following men were: Dr. W. E. Munsey, R. N. Havens, John G. Helvey, Watson Helvey, L. K. McNeil, S. V. Morris, J. D. Wright, W. R. Miller, J. M. Sheppard, Morris C. Miller, James Miller, Howard Miller, Bascom Miller, I. N. Munsey, Harris Bogle, Rufus Wheeler, P. P. Tabor, William Lambert—twenty in all.

"The above list was handed me by my life-long friend, Wm. Wright, and he made the following remark: 'I have seen all these preachers except Dr. Munsey, and have heard nearly all of them preach many times.' No wonder there have been no divorce cases. May the record never be broken."

Dr. Wagner was approaching his eightieth birthday when he gave us this account. He said that the site of the Kimberlin campground was on what was known as the Compton place, where Esca Mitchell lived when he wrote us. Dr. Wagner adds that he does not know how long these meetings were held, nor can he find anyone that does, but he is equally certain that none were held after the Civil War.

"The measure of success or how many conversions I do not know," says Dr. Wagner, "but Dr. William E. Munsey was converted there, and also Major W. N. Harman. I never saw Munsey, but he became one of our greatest pulpit orators. I knew Harman well; he has been in my home many times, and was one of the members of the first class of graduates of Emory & Henry College; he studied law, and became a very prominent lawyer, went to Texas and was General Sam Houston's legal adviser for some times. He enlisted in the Civil War as a major, and after the war was over he came to Holly Brook, his old home, and continued to practice law. He was always a very active church member."

Writing of Robert Sayers Sheffey he said, "He has been in my home many times. He was the best Christian man I ever knew."

Many years after the destruction of the buildings at the Wabash campground by fire there were evidences of the "power of God" in almost every religious service. And even today, many years later, we are told, the influences of those great meetings may be felt in that community.

Some years ago, Rev. George M. Moreland, for many years a member of the Holston conference, told the writer about an experience he had while preaching at a district conference at the Methodist church in that neighborhood about the year 1906-7. He had been appointed to preach at 3 o'clock in the afternoon, and the congregation had grown to be rather sluggish and sleepy-eyed. When he began his message people were nodding all over the house and the first fifteen minutes were exceedingly difficult. In a moment an air of expectancy seemed to grip the large audience and in a short time men and women were weeping and shouting all over the place. Religious emotions were stirred and the "fire" was burning in scores of hearts. The preacher was compelled to sit down and wait until the tides of joy were calmed before he could even attempt to pursue the delivery of his sermon. In a brief time the same thing happened the second time and shouts were heard in every direction. It was another out-pouring of the Holy Spirit, and men and women gave expression to the joys of the Christian religion. The message was never finished. The Spirit "preached" through lips of clay and there was power in His truth to stir human hearts.

Brother Morland, in reciting the story, said that in all his forty-odd years of experience as a Methodist preacher he had never seen so much shouting at a church service. This incident happened at the Eaton's Chapel meeting house.

Reference has been made elsewhere in these writings to the conversion and ministry of the sainted William E. Munsey, "that wonderful eloquent prodigy of the American pulpit." Munsey was a product of the old-fashioned camp meeting as were many others of the outstanding preachers of early Methodism. Munsey's spiritual father was George Stewart who came with his parents from Ireland in his infancy to Giles county, Va. Stewart, like Munsey, experienced his "new birth" at a camp meeting service held at the Old Wabash Camp Ground on August 7, 1841. Stewart was a great preacher. Dr. R. N. Price in his "History of Holston Methodism" says of him that he was a "man that deserves a book" in order that the whole story of his life might be told. Stewart proved to be a great preacher as well as a strong organizer. Telling of his first years, Dr. Price has this to say: "In 1849 he was a junior supply on his home work, traveling 200 miles each round, much of it over mere paths that were originally Indian and buffalo trails, much of it over almost impossible barriers, filling twenty-eight regular appointments, encountering floods, cold, and poverty, absent from home three weeks at a time, and rarely at home more than two days in succession. His salary was forty-one dollars, and it was the happiest period of his life up-to-date. The next year he traveled the Pearisburg circuit in the same relation, with about the same success. The most notable event of the year was his preaching on a Sunday evening at Kimberlin Camp Ground, just established, and finding in the rear of the congregation, among "the slain of the Lord," a youth whom he almost carried to the altar, and who was that night happily converted and afterwards became the wonder of our pulpit —namely, William E. Munsey." Stewart died in 1891. He was the father-in-law of Rev. John L. M. French, a Methodist preacher, and the grandfather of Rev. J. Stewart French, a leading figure in the Methodist church for many years.

Chapter XIII

"Twilight Is Stealing"

"How beautiful it is for a man to die
Upon the walls of Zion! to be called
Like a watchworn and weary sentinel,
To put his armour off, and rest in Heaven."
—Willis—"On Death of a Missionary"

It is evening time! The sunset hour is approaching! "The Courier of the Long Trail" is coming to the end of the trail toward which he has been traveling for eighty-two years. It is the hour of dissolution for the body as well as the moment of triumph for the soul. Anxious friends stand about the room eager to catch the last words of the old soldier of the Cross and to share in the untrammeled joy of his victorious soul.

The calendar reads August 30, 1902. The fingers of the clock pointed toward the figure 2. It is 2 o'clock in the afternoon. The whole earth is filled with glory. Supernal beauties are all about. The trees wave their leafy arms and shout for joy. Adown the valleys and across the mountains nature has bedecked herself in robes of richest glory and colors of green. It is a glorious day for the passing of a glorious soul.

There are shadows high on the hillsides come to mark the passing of another day. But there were no shadows across the pathway that lay ahead for Robert Sayers Sheffey, God's nobleman and Christian patriot.

Only a few friends are there to witness the passing of this saint. Those present were G. T. Whitaker, J. Calvin Vest, and Aurelius Vest and family. Members of his own immediate family did not arrive until several hours later.

For several years Brother Sheffey had been living at the home of Aurelius Vest until it had come to be like second home to him. His own home had been left behind after the passing of his companion. His son, Edward F. Sheffey, living in Lynchburg, had urged him to come and be with him, but his father never cared very much for the city and its busy life. Rather he preferred to live among the hills where he had spent so many happy years and among the people who were almost as dear to him as his own loved ones. His first family had already scattered in different sections of Southwest Virginia and since the larger part of his life had been lived in Giles county, it was here that he wanted to spend his last days among his friends.

Aurelius Vest lived about two miles west of White Gate. He owned a home facing Lewey's mountain, on the north. He engaged in farming and for many years conducted the work of a country undertaker. His was a modest home, but it was a home where the members of the family reverenced God and believed and practiced the tenets of the Christian religion in their daily lives. They were a happy and contented family and the worship of God was inherent in their very souls. It was in an atmosphere of this nature that Brother Sheffey elected to spend his last days.

After more than a half century of arduous toil in the Master's Kingdom this beloved man set his face to go to this home where those who labored to care for him during the last months of his life performed those "labors of love" with the tenderest hands and most patient souls possible under the circumstances.

Thirty years after his death the writer visited the old Vest home and as the spot where he died was pointed out there were tears in the eyes of the members of the family who were present. The memory of that "man of God" lingered like a sacred benediction about that household even to that late day. We were then shown the bedstead upon which he died and this caused the tears to spring afresh to those eyes that wept at his going away.

One day Mr. Vest was preparing a coffin for some neighbor. That was in the days when coffins were made by hand in community work-shops. Brother Sheffey happened by while at the Vest home and he remarked to the undertaker that he wanted to see the coffin when it was finished. When the work had been completed Vest told him that he could go down to his shop and look at it. Sheffey remarked, "It won't be long before I shall need one. My work is almost done. I've changed my mind. I don't think I care to see it." This was several years before his death.

Mr. Vest made the coffin in which Brother Sheffey was buried. It was made of solid walnut and was made several weeks before his death for a "stock" casket. The suggestion of the type of casket to be used for Brother Sheffey was made by his son, Edward F. Sheffey.

Edward Sheffey made frequent visits to see his father. A son by his first marriage, James Sheffey of Marion, also visited him during his last illness. The other members of his family did not get to visit him too often because of the lack of transportation facilities. It was not as easy to travel in those days as now. When they wrote him it was always with the tenderest of feelings and with every evidence of love and affection.

Edward Sheffey sought to make the last days of his father as comfortable as possible. He contributed to his support and saw that Mr. Vest was repaid for the trouble and time spent in caring for his father during his last illness. A number of letters in possession of the writer reveals the love and tender affection upon the part of the son for his father.

The following letter was written from Lynchburg on July 2, 1902, two days before the anniversary of his eighty-second birthday. It is copied in full:

"My dear, dear Father:

"This is your birthday letter—July 4th—and so you are eighty-two years old today. God bless you on this your natal day. Truly God has been good to you and I know you are grateful to Him for all His loving kindness and tender mercy.

"I am sending you by express today a box of lemons, cakes, candy, etc. The Seay family send the big round one with their love. Mrs. Gardner will attend to sending the package over to White Gate. I hope it will reach you on the 4th.

"I enclose a check for $5.00. Have Aurelius use it to buy anything you may wish and desire. Perhaps you might wish to give some of it to some of the dear children or people there. Do as you wish. Aurelius will cash it for you. Wish I could be with you on the 4th but cannot well make it. Pray for me.

"I received two letters Aurelius wrote 27th and 30th of

June. Thank him for me. Tell him to write me again on the 4th of July. You send me a message and let him put down what you say, please sir.

"Again God bless you on your birthday.

"Our love to all the people there.

"Your loving son,
"E. F. Sheffey."

This letter was written just two months before Brother Sheffey's death and reveals something of the tender ties that there were between father and son. It also speaks volumes of words that human tongues can never utter.

The latter days of Robert Sayers Sheffey were filled with pain and intense suffering at times. Dr. J. E. Blackburn, of White Gate, attended him during his illness which covered exactly seven months and twelve days. He suffered a great deal with rheumatic condition which had followed a long and active life in the service of the Lord and humanity across the hill country and Southwestern Virginia and Southern West Virginia.

The circumstances under which he died were related to the writer by Mr. Vest as he stood with tear-dimmed eyes and thought of those days preceding his passing. On the evening before he died, while the Vest family were at supper, Brother Sheffey became gloriously happy. He exclaimed, "The prettiest and brightest things I have ever seen. How beautiful and bright my star is. I have got in a good way. The sweet angels. Praise the Lord. Praise the Lord. Praise the Lord. So happy. So happy. Tell Eddy to praise the Lord."

And then he slowly lapsed into unconsciousness and remained in that condition until the end came.

A great many visitors came to be with him during his illness and he would have someone read the Scriptures and offer a prayer even after he grew to be so weak that he could scarcely speak above a whisper. Shortly before his death he called a member of the Vest family to his bedside and had them to write some of his thoughts. I have the words before me now. They were: "Truly God is good and His tender mercies are over all His works. Blessed are they that seek after true riches, for theirs is the kingdom of heaven. Praise the Lord, O, my soul; praise His holy name;

let all the people praise Thy matchless and highly exalted name, for praise is comely among saints. Make a joyful noise all ye that love Him. Let everything that breathes praise Him."

"The Lord is our light and our salvation and in Him is no darkness. The Lord has promised never to leave us nor forsake us. Glory to His name."

"We ought to be careful not to grieve our sweet Friend, our Saviour; let us love Him and be patient to keep His commandments forevermore. Praise Him. Praise Him."

His life even to the end was filled with praise and thanksgiving to God who had traveled with him all those eventful and useful years of his life. He had made preparation as against this very experience. He knew the full meaning of that immortal poem, "Thanatopsis," written by William Cullen Bryant:

> "So live that when thy summons comes to join
> The innumerable caravan, that moves
> To the pale realm of shade, where each shall take
> His chamber in the silent halls of death,
> Thou go not, like the quarry-slave at night
> Scourged to his dungeon; but, sustained and soothed
> By an unfaltering trust, approach thy grave,
> Like one who wraps the drapery of his couch
> About him, and lies down to pleasant dreams."

Quiet in soul and body he approached the inevitable issue of life—death. And he visualized something of the joys of that Eternal City, that "house not made with hands," as he exclaimed, "The prettiest and brightest thing I have ever seen." No wonder that he shouted in those passing moments, "Praise the Lord."

An Australian writer tells of an awful night in Scotland: "The snow was deep; the wind simply shrieked around the little hut in which a good old elder lay dying. His daughter brought the family Bible to his bedside. 'Father,' she said, 'will I read a chapter to ye?' But the elder was in sore pain and only moaned. She opened the Book. 'Na, na, lassie,' he said, 'the storm's up noo; I theekit (thatched) ma hoose in the calm weather.' ". That's what

Robert Sayers Sheffey had done, and as the hour of dissolution drew near he was able to say, "I am so happy."

The funeral of Brother Sheffey was very largely attended by people from all over Southwest Virginia and Southern West Virginia. They came in wagons, buggies, on foot, horseback, and in every available conveyance. People came because they wanted to pay tribute to a man whose life had been lived above reproach. They came because they wanted to mingle their tears with those who sorrowed and because they felt a very keen sense of personal loss—the loss of a friend, a brother, a Christian adviser, God's nobleman, soldier of the Cross, a disciple of Christ, a man who went about doing good like his Master. No wonder they inscribed upon his monument the words, "The poor were sorry when he died."

The Wesley's Chapel church, at Trigg, in Giles county, on the Eggleston charge of the Holston conference, was the scene of his funeral. The building was packed with people and many were standing on the outside while the services were being conducted by Rev. Chaffin Crockett, his pastor and friend of many years. Others participating in the service were the Rev. George A. Maiden, presiding elder of the Radford district, and Rev. Eugene Blake, pastor of the Pearisburg Methodist church. The body was laid to rest in the beautiful cemetery surrounding the church building. There he sleeps beside the body of Eliza Stafford Sheffey to await the second coming of His Lord and Master.

More than fifty years have elapsed since he went away, but his grave is visited yearly by throngs of people who want to look upon the place where he sleeps his last long sleep. They come with uncovered heads and whisper as they stand about his tomb. Their eyes are wet with tears as they recall his memory.

What could be more fitting than to append here the songs that he sang so often during his active ministry, songs that took on a different meaning as he came near to the crossing of the river of death?

> "Twilight is stealing over the sea,
> Shadows are falling dark on the lea;
> Bourne on the night-winds, voices of yore
> Come from the far-off shore.

Refrain

Far away beyond the star-lit skies,
Where the love-light never, never dies,
Gleameth a mansion, filled with delight,
Sweet, happy home so bright.

Voices of loved ones! songs of the past!
Still linger round me while life shall last;
Lonely I wander, sadly I roam,
Seeking that far-off home.

Come in the twilight, come, come to me!
Bringing some message over the sea,
Cheering my pathway while here I roam,
Seeking that far-off home.

What more appropriate words than those of St. Paul could be appended at the close of this life? "The time of my departure is at hand, I have fought a good fight, I have finished my course, I have kept the faith: henceforth there is laid up for me a crown of righteousness, which the Lord, the righteous judge, shall give me at that day."

"My latest sun is sinking fast,
My race is nearly run,
My strongest trials now are past,
My triumph is begun.

Refrain

"O come, angel band, come and around me stand,
O bear me away on your snowy wings
To my immortal home;
O bear me away on your snowy wings
To my immortal home.

"I know I am nearing the holy ranks
Of friends and kindred dear;
I brush the dews on Jordan's banks,
The crossing must be near.

"I've almost gained my heavenly home,
My spirit loudly sings.
The holy ones, behold they come;
I hear the noise of wings.

"O bear my longing heart to Him,
Who bled and died for me,
Whose blood now cleanses from all sin,
And gives me victory.

The Bluefield Daily Telegraph of Friday morning, September 5th, 1902, carried the story of the funeral in these words: Soldier of the Cross and Child of Faith. Remarkable Incidents in the Career of the Rev. Robert Sayers Sheffey, Well Known Throughout Southwest Virginia as a Man of Prayer. The funeral services of the late Rev. Robert Sayers Sheffey were held at Wesley's Chapel in Giles county in the presence of an immense concourse of friends from many counties. Rev. R. F. Jackson, pastor of the Staffordsville circuit, conducted the services assisted by Rev. G. A. Maiden, D. D., presiding elder of the Radford district, and Rev. Eugene Blake, pastor of the Pearisburg circuit.

The funeral sermon was preached by Rev. W. C. Crockett, of the Bland circuit. He said in substance: "Robert Sayers Sheffey was a man gentle and refined, both by nature and grace. He was wont to say, 'I was born naturally and the son of Henry Sheffey and Margaret White, July 4, 1820, in Wythe county, Virginia, near Ivanhoe, and was born of the Spirit January 9, 1839, in the third story of John C. Greenway's store house in the town of Abingdon.' He was pre-eminently a man of faith. He literally left all and followed Christ. He prayed to God in faith, and God heard and answered his prayers. He did his duty. He was faithful. During his long illness, extending over a period of many long months, not a day passed but that he had family prayers in the kind home which sheltered and shielded him, and when too weak to pray, he would ask or signal others to pray. Among his last words were these, 'The prettiest and brightest things I have seen. How beautiful and bright my star. I am in a good way. The sweet angels. Praise the Lord, praise the Lord; tell Eddy to praise the Lord,' and with these thoughts and visions he quickly sank to rest and sleep, as a little child to wake in heaven."

Dr. Maiden believed that he had never seen or met anyone of like faith. No one had so projected his life on the hearts and consciences of the masses of Southwestern Virginia and Southern West Virginia as he had, and he believed that Brother Sheffey had never entered a home or touched a life but that blessings had come therefrom. He believed in God's cause and gave not only all his time without stipulated compensation, but gave more money than many worth thousands, and cited an instance where in a service on a circuit he contributed at every church to missions, and subscribed more than the richest man on the bluegrass circuit, and the evening before the pastor in charge started for conference, months afterwards, Brother Sheffey rode up and made settlement of all he had subscribed. He never forgot his obligations, and discharged them all.

Rev. Mr. Blake testified to the love of the deceased for the poor, and gave illustration of a visit with him to a mountain cabin, in dead of winter, where dwelt a very poor and helpless, but good man. During the conversation, Brother Sheffey excused himself, came back in a few moments and placed something in the old man's pockets. The preacher afterwards charged him with having taken off his own woven wool socks and giving them to the poor man. Said he, "Brother, the Lord told me to do it. He needed them more than I do, and He will take care of me." And He did, for though not possessed of the means of this world, he never lacked for anything.

His enmity to the liquor traffic was referred to by Mr. Blake and Dr. Maiden, and remarkable cases of the annihilation of distilleries in direct answer to his prayers were cited. Mention was made of his having at times spent hours in prayer for the sick, of whose recovery no hope was entertained by the doctors, with the result that the sick lived.

The exercises were concluded by Rev. Mr. Jackson at the grave, where all that was mortal of this true "Soldier of the Cross and Follower of the Lamb" were laid to rest by the side of his beloved wife, and while sweet songs, the songs he loved so well, were floating out on the summer's breeze, loving hands placed beautiful flowers upon the new-made grave and bathed them with their tears.

"We live in deeds, not years; in thoughts, not breaths; in feelings, not in figures on a dial; we should count time by heart throbs. He most lives who thinks most, feels the noblest, acts the best."

"Servant of God, well done; rest in peace."